Stalking and Violence

Stalking and Violence
New Patterns of Trauma and Obsession

Stephen J. Morewitz

*Stephen J. Morewitz, Ph.D., & Associates
and Chair, Crime and Delinquency Division
The Society for the Study of Social Problems*

Kluwer Academic / Plenum Publishers
New York Boston Dordrecht London Moscow

Magale Library
Southern Arkansas University
Magnolia, Arkansas 71753

DISCARD

Library of Congress Cataloging-in-Publication Data

Morewitz, Stephen John, 1954–
  Stalking and violence: new patterns of trauma and obsession/Stephen J. Morewitz.
    p.   cm.
  Includes bibliographical references and index.
  ISBN 0-306-47365-8
    1. Stalking—United States.   2. Stalkers—United States—Psychology.   3. Stalking
  victims—United States.   I. Title.

HV6594.2 .M67 2002
362.88—dc21
                                                                    2002028689

ISBN 0-306-47365-8

© 2003 Kluwer Academic / Plenum Publishers, New York
233 Spring Street, New York, New York 10013

http://www.wkap.nl/

10 9 8 7 6 5 4 3 2

A C.I.P. record for this book is available from the Library of Congress

Preface

The concept of stalking, e.g., repeated and unwanted following, lying in wait, and other intrusive and harassing behaviors, did not come into public consciousness until the late 1980s (Meloy, 1999). The stalking of President Ronald Reagan, Rebecca Schaeffer, Jodie Foster, David Letterman, and Nicole Simpson were high-profile examples (Dietz, et al., 1991a; Dietz, et al., 1991b). The media played an instrumental role in transforming stalking into a social problem. Movies such as, Fatal Attraction, television and radio broadcasts, and the print media brought into public awareness the deadly consequences of stalking and the frustration and helplessness of stalking victims (Lowney & Best, 1995, pp. 33–57).

Stalking is not a new phenomenon; in fact, a sub-type of stalking, erotomania, has been known and documented in ancient times. Erotomanics stalk their targets to fulfill a delusional belief or fantasy that their target is in love with them (Esquirol, 1838; de Clerambault, 1921; Zona, et al., 1993; Kurt, 1995, p. 223). Other stalkers hold paranoid and other delusional beliefs and will stalk and attempt to harm their targets as a result of these delusional beliefs (Dietz, et al., 1991a; Dietz, et al., 1991b). The stalking syndrome is not limited to erotomania and other severe pathologies, but encompasses many "normal" persons who for various reasons stalk their dates, acquaintances, spouses, and other family members (NIJ, 1998; Kurt, 1995, p. 225; Hamburger & Hastings, 1986).

The 1989 murder of Rebecca Schaeffer led to the enactment of the first anti-stalking law in California in 1990. California's anti-stalking statute became a model for other states. Public outcry over stalking led to U. S. Congressional hearings and the enactment of anti-stalking laws at the state and federal levels. Community-based and Internet-based organizations were formed to deal with the problems posed by stalkers. The federal government established a model stalking code to assist states in developing constitutional and enforceable laws. The increased access to the Internet also resulted in public concern about stalkers, pedophiles, and other predators online, and twenty-six states now have laws against electronic stalking.

Along with the development of stalking as a social problem and its inclusion into the realm of legal problems, came research into the sociology and psychology of stalking (NIJ, 1998; Emerson, et al., 1998, pp. 289–314; Meloy, 1998; Meloy, 1999; Lowney & Best, 1995, pp. 33–57; Boychuk, 1994). The National Institute of Justice-supported National Violence Against Women survey estimated that 8% of women and 2% of men in the U.S. are stalked at one time in their life, while 1% of women and 0.4% of men are stalked annually (NIJ, 1998). Research has focused on clinical evaluations of perpetrators, analysis of stalking in current and/or terminated relationships, and legal analysis of stalking and the criminal justice system (Sinclair & Frieze, 2000, p. 24; Brewster, 2000, pp. 41–54; Spitzberg, Nicastro, & Cousins, 1998; Boychuk, 1994). In addition, in this book, quantitative and qualitative findings from the Stalking and Violence Project (SVP) will describe new patterns and effects of stalking in social relationships using a random sample of 519 protective orders filed in two domestic courts (See Appendix A—Research Methods and Appendix B—Selected Cases from the Stalking and Violence Project).

With the enactment of anti-stalking laws, domestic courts are now collecting data on stalking incidents. These analyses of domestic court cases will provide invaluable insights into the dynamics and impact of stalking in different relationships and the response of the police, courts, and mental health professionals to stalking complaints.

One of the central assumptions in this book is that stalking is a patterned set of behaviors that arises out of attempts to exert power over other persons in a variety of relationships. Stalkers use stalking behaviors to develop and maintain relationships, retaliate, and/or punish those whom they perceive as having hurt them. In this way, stalking becomes an essential aspect of forming, maintaining, and ending various types of relationships in the mind of the stalker (Emerson, et al., 1998).

This book also assesses the extent to which gender, age, and other characteristics of victims and offenders affect the patterns of stalking behaviors. This process will shed light on the degree to which the roles and norms related to demographic and social characteristics influence the dynamics of stalking as well as the diverse and sometimes ambiguous nature of stalking itself (Tjaden, Thoesnnes, & Allison, 2000, pp. 7–22).

First, some researchers assert that stalking can involve a variety of behaviors, e.g., following, lying in wait, telephoning a person at home or work, and assaults (Sinclair & Frieze, 2000, pp. 23–35; Brewster, 2000, pp. 41–54). Some of these actions, when viewed in isolation, may not seem to qualify as stalking.

Second, stalking varies in severity from being a mild nuisance to being extremely stressful and dangerous. Motivations underlying stalking behaviors may affect the severity of the phenomenon. For instance, stalking that is motivated by jealousy and anger may be more violent than stalking that is guided by other motivations.

Third, the duration of stalking varies and when the time frame is short, neither the victim nor the perpetrator may consider the behavior as stalking.

Fourth, certain social norms encourage some forms of stalking as legitimate behavior and, this blurs the line between stalking and legitimate behaviors. Sinclair and Frieze (2000) describe how courtship norms, e.g., "at first you don't succeed try, try again," encourage suitors to pursue their love objects even when the targets explicitly rejects them. Movies such as The Graduate and There's Something About Mary exemplify the fine line between courtship persistence and stalking. The pursuer's behaviors initially may be perceived by the love object as normal courtship behaviors, which gradually evolve into being a nuisance, and ultimately to stalking.

Fifth, persons have made false claims of being stalked, which contribute to skepticism about the authenticity of claims made by stalking victims (Mohandie, Hatcher & Raymond, 1998).

The book evaluates the diverse and sometimes ambiguous nature of stalking in terms of its demographic and social patterns, psychological consequences, and organizational reactions.

Chapter 1 explores the types of relationships in which stalking occurs and which factors are related to stalking and violence in these relationships.

Chapter 2 describes stalking in terms of a technological innovation in communication: the electronic stalking of children and adults. The impact of increased Internet use on patterns of electronic stalking and organizational responses to electronic stalking are assessed.

In Chapter 3, the demographic and social characteristics of offenders and victims are analyzed to determine the degree to which power dynamics in the larger society influence patterns of stalking, control, and violence. The possible effects of gender, age, and race/ethnicity are elucidated.

Chapter 4 investigates the social, psychological, and economic impact of stalking in different social relationships. Emphasis is on the power inequities between stalkers and their victims and the ineffectiveness of the criminal justice system, both of which can result in severe stress and trauma for stalking victims.

In Chapter 5, the focus is on the informal, non-legal approaches that stalking victims take in dealing with their stalkers. The victims' responses to their perpetrators and their use of safety precautions, domestic violence shelters, and mental health services are analyzed.

The enactment of anti-stalking laws and the victims' use of the courts are assessed in Chapter 6. Emphasis is placed on the societal conditions that gave rise to anti-stalking legislation, the elements of anti-stalking laws, their constitutionality, and factors associated with the stalking victims' requests for protective orders.

Chapter 7 describes the conditions under which stalking victims and others seek police assistance to resolve stalking incidents. The characteristics of victims and offenders in different relationships are evaluated to determine which factors are related to seeking police assistance for stalking incidents.

The classification of stalkers for psychosocial treatment and/or incarceration are explored in Chapter 8. This chapter focuses on effective treatment for victims and their perpetrators and which conditions are associated with successful treatment outcomes for victims and offenders.

Finally, in the last chapter, the book analyzes the implications of stalking in face-to-face interactions and in society.

Acknowledgments

This book would not have been completed without the advice and support of many people. I would like to thank Dr. Lloyd Klein, Dr. J. Barry Gurdin, Mrs. Myra Kalkin Morewitz, and Dr. Harry A. Morewitz for their advice and support. I also want to thank Sharon Panulla, Clinical Psychology Editor at Kluwer Academic/Plenum Publishers, and Sarah Williams, Editorial Assistant at Kluwer, who have been supportive as well as thorough and thoughtful.

Contents

1

Stalking and Role Relationships

Researchers are beginning to study stalking in different role relationships to see how stalking and related behaviors may be affected. Stalking can develop and persist as persons try to resolve relationship problems associated with dating, marriage, and interactions with relatives.

Individuals with attachment difficulties and a history of failed relationships are apt to become stalkers as they attempt to deal with their social losses (Cupach & Spitzberg, 1998, p. 249; Meloy, 1996, p. 151; Meloy & Gothard, 1995, p. 261). Violent criminals, others with a history of violence, and persons who threaten former intimates are also likely to engage in stalking and violent behaviors (Brewster, 2000, pp. 41–54).

Persons who are predisposed to stalking are either limited or encouraged by various role-specific norms, values, and expectations. Spouses may stalk their partners if they suspect that they are committing adultery or neglecting their children. In dating relationships, the media emphasis on the proactive male role may actually encourage date stalking (Sinclair & Frieze, 2000, pp. 23–55).

Moreover, societal expectations may influence the ways in which victims perceive and respond to stalking. Because of marital customs, expectations, and values, marriage partners may not perceive behaviors as stalking even though it would be considered as such in other social contexts. These victims, therefore, may not develop the same stress-related health and negative social effects that occur when the behaviors are perceived as aberrant.

In addition, sexual orientation, ethnic background, socioeconomic status, age, and other social characteristics of the individuals may affect the process and content of stalking in various roles. For instance, the perception of date and/or spouse stalking may vary depending on a person's age, ethnic background, and socioeconomic status. In this context, ethnic norms and values, such as the Latino values of machismo, may guide the extent to which a person uses stalking as a control mechanism.

Stranger and Acquaintance Stalking

In stranger stalking, the offender and victim do not know each other, whereas in acquaintance stalking, the victim knows the stalker on a casual basis. Victims and offenders may be co-workers, neighbors, or fellow members of a social organization. Thus, acquaintance stalking can involve diverse roles and motivations. Individuals may stalk and harass their neighbors due to residential disputes over excessive noise, obnoxious trash, and offensive landscaping. Offenders also may stalk and harass a neighbor or co-worker because they wish to develop an intimate relationship or are seeking revenge for a real or imagined injustice.

To what extent are stranger and acquaintance stalking linked to physical violence? There have been a number of publicized cases of stranger stalking that resulted in violence and death. The 1989 murder of Rebecca Schaeffer, a Hollywood actress, led to the development of anti-stalking laws. There is ample evidence that violence by both men and women occurs across different role relationships, especially in dating and intimate relationships. Yet, the link between stalking and violence in stranger and acquaintance relationships has not been well delineated. In terms of prevalence data, there are little data on the relationship between stranger stalking and violence in the general population.

The largest study to date, the National Violence Against Women (NVAW) survey of 8,000 women and 8,000 men found that stalking was positively related to violence in intimate relations.

Moreover, in the NVAW Survey, 45% of the female victims and 43% of the male victims who were stalked by all types of stalkers were overtly threatened by their stalkers (NIJ, 1998, p. 13). However, the NVAW survey did not discuss whether stranger and acquaintance stalking resulted in physical assaults against the stalking victims. In a study of individuals who threatened members of the U.S. Congress, Dietz, et al. (1991) reported that persons who threatened members of Congress were less likely to approach their targets than those offenders who did not threaten the Congress person but did stalk them (Dietz, et al., 1991, pp. 1459–1460).

The risks of physical violence from stranger stalking may be a function of the psychopathology of the offender since the stranger stalker is the primary source of the stalking and violence. In contrast, violence related to acquaintance stalking may be due, in part, to the level of familiarity between the offender and victim. As acquaintances become more familiar with each other, there are more opportunities for conflict and violence. With greater familiarity between the offender and victim, the interactions begin to resemble violent dating relationships. Additional research is needed to determine the relationship between stranger/acquaintance stalking and physical violence.

The NVAW Survey found that over a lifetime women are more likely than men to be stalked by strangers and acquaintances (NIJ, p. 12). The NVAW report also found that 90% of the offenders who engaged in stranger and acquaintance stalking are male. According to the NVAW report, it is not known why male victims are stalked by male strangers and male acquaintances. However, there is evidence that homosexual men are more likely than heterosexual men to be stalked by male strangers and acquaintances (NIJ, 1998, pp. 11–12).

In addition to quantitative investigations, more case studies are needed to clarify the social milieu of acquaintance stalking and the impact of these behaviors on the social and psychological well-being of the victims. The SVP Case10C illustrates how acquaintance stalking can result in both physical violence and significant stress to the victim and her/his family (See Appendix B). In SVP Case 10C, Mr. C complained of repeated harassment and stalking by Mr. D, a 42-year-old male who lived in the same building. Mr. C reported that when the offender had verbally assaulted him on three occasions, he called the police. The police came to Mr. D's apartment, and the offender had promised to move away and stop the cursing, but he did not do so. That same year, Mr. D came to the victim's residence and ordered the children to awaken their father. The perpetrator then cursed and physically assaulted Mr. C in the hallway of their apartment. Mr. C sustained bruises to his kidney and back and reported that he and the rest of his family were traumatized by the attack.

Date Stalking

Researchers are now beginning to evaluate the prevalence and nature of date stalking. The NVAW Survey found that 14% of the female stalking victims had been stalked by a current or former boyfriend or date (NIJ, 1998, p. 6). The SVP found that 36% of stalking victims were or have been in dating relationships with the offenders. The higher percentage of date stalking in the SVP may reflect the higher prevalence of date stalking among victims who have filed orders of protection, as compared to individuals who participated in a nationally representative telephone survey.

Date stalking frequently is motivated by a desire to form a relationship or maintain a failed one as well as by revenge and vindictiveness over the ending of a relationship. Persons with attachment difficulties are especially vulnerable because they do not have the psychological and social resources to deal with failures in forming or maintaining social relationships. They will respond with emotional and physical abuse and violence over social losses that threaten their self-esteem and identity. Although research in this area is scant, it is likely that persons who stalk their dates may have personality disorders. Date stalkers may be similar to spouse stalkers who suffer from various personality disorders (Kurt, 1995, p. 225).

Individuals with a violent criminal history and those with a history of substance abuse are likely to be involved in date stalking (Cupach & Spitzberg, 1998, p. 249; McReynolds, 1996, p. 41). These persons are predisposed to engage in stalking behaviors as part of their on-going patterns of breaking the law. Moreover, a person may initiate and maintain stalking behaviors because of a deterioration in their functioning brought on by certain forms of substance abuse. Hall (1996)'s study of stalking victims found that those persons with a history of committing violence, who grew up in violent families, and previously had stalked other people were likely to be stalkers. These findings support the literature on the cycle of violence that show how violent families facilitate the intergenerational transmission of violence.

Although date stalkers may have a violent history and come from violent families, the association between date stalking and physical violence has not been explored fully. The NVAW Survey did not address this issue directly; their study emphasized stalking and violence by current or former husbands or cohabiting partners (NIJ, 1998, p. 14). Cupach and Spitzberg (1998) assert that obsessed estranged lovers as a group may be the most dangerous stalkers (Cupach & Spitzberg, 1998, p. 248).

However, violence committed by current or former dates may vary depending on their level of intimacy and emotional involvement with the victims. Other social characteristics of the offenders and victims also may affect the degree to which date stalking is related to violence.

Several cases from the SVP demonstrate that date stalking is positively linked to verbal threats. Date stalking and harassment are precipitated by threats or actual break-ups of dating relationships. Revenge and persecution by a woman who was in a former dating relationship is reflected in SVP Case 424C. Mr. G reported that his former date, Ms. H, a 21-year-old woman, had threatened him and his family with physical harm. On another occasion, Mr. G called the police when Ms. H came to his home and kicked in his windows. The victim currently receives many threatening calls at work from Ms. H, which has adversely affected his concentration on the job and caused him to fear for his safety.

SVP Case 326C demonstrates how date stalking can be initiated when a woman announces her desires to break up with her boyfriend. One night, Ms. I, a single, 22-year-old woman, handed a "Dear John" letter to her boyfriend, Mr. J. After reading it, he became distraught, jumped out of the window of his home, and began to chase Ms. I. Mr. J took her car keys and grabbed her by both arms, causing her considerable pain. The man would not allow Ms. I to leave. Eight hours later, they had a conversation again, and she agreed not to break up with him. Mr. J finally allowed her to leave his home.

Spouse Stalking

Spouses who stalk their partners may do so to try to reconcile their marriages. In other instances, married partners stalk as a way of retaliating against their spouses. Spouses may also stalk their partners because of jealousy or to ascertain if they have been cheating on them, taking care of their children properly or performing other family responsibilities. The stalkers may be anticipating a divorce or seeking custody of the children and stalking their partners to collect evidence.

SVP Case 285C demonstrates how a spouse used stalking in an attempt to salvage a marriage. In this case, Mrs. M reported that her husband, Mr. N, a 61-year-old man, who was living at a different residence, repeatedly called her home and workplace and threatened to kill her if she did not take him back. Mrs. M stated that she is stressed out and cannot sleep at night because her husband has keys to her house.

According to the NVAW Survey, 38% of the female victims reported being stalked by a current or former spouse (NIJ, 1998, p. 10). The results from the SVP revealed that 25% of the current spouses who filed orders of protection against their spouses reported being stalked by their current spouses. The lower percentage of spouse stalking in the SVP may be due to the fact that the category, "current spouse," was used rather than combining current and former spouses in a single category. Former spouses may be more likely than current spouses to stalk to force a reconciliation, monitor their former partners' activities, and retaliate against them.

To what extent is spouse stalking also related to domestic violence? It is important to note that both husbands and wives face physical violence in marital relations. In fact, some research has shown that a higher percentage of wives than husbands have used physical violence in marital relationships (Steinmetz, 1977–1978, p. 499). The NVAW findings support the studies that show that current or former husbands are more likely than wives to use physical violence against their partners. Moreover, the husbands' use of physical violence is linked to stalking their wives. According to the NVAW Survey, stalking by current or former husbands is significantly related to physical violence against the wives. Eighty-one percent of the women who were stalked by a current or former spouse also reported being physically assaulted by him (NIJ, 1998, p. 6). The NVAW survey also found that 45% of the female stalking victims and 45% of the male stalking victims were overtly threatened by their offenders.

The quantitative results from the SVP showed that among married Hispanic and White offenders, stalking was positively related to throwing down the victims. In contrast, among married African-American offenders, there was no relationship between stalking and physical violence against the partners.

To what degree is spouse stalking also related to sexual assaults against partners? Do husbands who sexually assault and rape their wives also stalk them? According to the NVAW Survey, 31% of the women who were stalked by a current or former spouse or cohabiting partner also were sexually assaulted by this same person (NIJ, 1998, p. 14). However, in the SVP, spouse stalking was negatively related to partner sexual assaults (Morewitz, 2001a). Additional investigations are needed to evaluate the possible link between stalking and sexual assaults of married partners.

Intimate Partner Stalking

Stalking also occurs among intimate, non-married partners. The NVAW Survey findings revealed that 10% of the female stalking victims indicated that they had been stalked by a current or former cohabiting partners (NIJ, 1998, p. 10). As noted previously, the NVAW study found that some female stalking victims are physically and sexually assaulted by their current or former cohabiting partners. Individuals who have been non-married intimate partners, like married persons, engage in stalking and harassment to try to reconcile their relationships, retaliate against the current or former partner, or monitor their partner's activities. Unlike married persons, non-married intimate partners do not have the same roles and expectations as married persons. However, in certain states, if they have lived together for a lengthy time period, they may be considered to be in a common-law marriage.

Family Member/Relative Stalking

Family and relative stalking is a new area of research involving various family problems and disputes. Family members with drug and alcohol problems may steal from other family members to support their addiction. In other cases, the stalkers who have engaged in other illegal enterprises, which resulted in their expulsion from the family home, may stalk other family members to retaliate or to get back into the residence. In other instances, family members may have a dispute and stalk other family members in order to retaliate or to monitor their activities.

What is the prevalence of family and relative stalking? The NVAW Survey found that 4% of women and 2% of men reported being stalked by a relative other than their spouse (NIJ, 1998, p. 11). The prevalence and nature of family and relative stalking have not been emphasized in other investigations. Case studies provide a good overview of family and relative stalking. Family stalking is illustrated by SVP Case # 377C in which Mrs. U was stalked by her 32-year-old son, Mr. V, who she claims has a drug problem. Mrs. U called the police one morning because her son was verbally abusing her and banging on one of her windows in an attempt to gain entrance into her house. The mother complained that her son had tried to get into her house a number of times before and also had damaged her home and car.

Conclusion

This analysis has found similarities and differences in stalking across different role relationships. A similarity is that in every relationship, stalking behavior is not a one time occurrence. Repeated intrusions in different roles are both psychological and symbolic as well as physical (Cupach & Spitzberg, 1998, p. 241). Second, the severity of stalking and harassment in each role varies from mild to severe. Stalking and harassment may start out as nuisances and become intolerable when repeated. Stalking victims often experience severe stresses associated with stalking in various roles, often experiencing stress-related health problems and major disruption of social, family, and occupational/educational functioning.

Stalking may be influenced by ethnic background and socio-economic status. For instance, the Latino values of machismo and marianismo emphasize male control and female subordination as well as family solidarity. These cultural values may encourage men to stalk women in dating and marital relationships as a way of maintaining control over them.

In regard to differences in stalking, the values, expectations, and norms associated with different roles may lead to variability in the frequency, process, and outcome of stalking and harassment. For example, dating roles that foster intense and repeated stalking and harassment may find the target acquiescing to the pursuer. In contrast, stranger stalking and family stalking do not have societal norms and expectations that guide stalking behaviors.

Offenders also use stalking and other forms of harassment in order to achieve various objectives, and these objectives vary depending on the role relationship. In date stalking, offenders use stalking in order to establish a new relationship, monitor their date's behaviors, restore a failing relationship, and take revenge against a date. In contrast, family and relative stalking are oriented toward family and relative disputes. In marital relations, stalking is used for monitoring a spouse's activities, especially during divorce and child custody disputes, ensuring the safety of the children, and taking revenge against the partner.

Violence related to stalking also may vary across roles. Violence associated with stalking may be more likely to occur in role relationships that are more intimate and long-term than stranger and acquaintance interactions. There are insufficient data to determine if stalking in association with physical violence is more likely to occur among family members and relatives than in other relationships.

Life course changes may influence the onset, frequency, and severity of stalking behaviors. For instance, people in certain age groups are expected to follow conventional expectations by being married and having children. As these societal expectations are disrupted by the break up of relationships, individuals will resort to stalking and other harassment to deal with these inappropriate disruptions of conventional life. Other life course changes may facilitate or inhibit stalking. For example, in the SVP, women who were pregnant were less likely to be stalked than non-pregnant women (Morewitz, 2001b).

This analysis has shown how the social context of different role relationships leads to differences in stalking and related behaviors. These findings show how role-specific norms, values and expectations facilitate or inhibit stalking behaviors over a person's life course. In this way, an offender's psychopathology can be directly influenced by role-specific values, norms, and expectations.

2

Cyberstalking

Child and Adult Victims

Between 1995 and 2000, access to the Internet grew extensively. Widespread use of this new and powerful technology unfortunately spawns attempts to abuse it. Stalkers are finding the Internet a powerful tool to aid them in their ability to stalk both children and adults. The public is now alarmed about protecting children as well as adults from online stalking.

Online Child Victims

Children have been victimized by online pornographers and pedophiles who "surf" children's chat rooms and then meet the children offline to engage in illegal sexual behaviors (NIJ, 1999, p. 2). The Internet offers social support to various predators who meet online and create web sites to transmit pornographic materials and share information and advice about how to stalk children and adult victims (Richardson, ABCNEWS.com, Feb. 13, 2001).

Because so-called cyberstalking is a recent phenomenon, there is little known about the prevalence of pedophiles on the web. According to FBI statistics, there are a total of 100 to 200 cases of children abducted by strangers per year (Kincaid, Salon.com, Aug. 24, 2000, pp. 1–5). These cases typically consist of the child being abducted and injured. The FBI does not have data on what percentage of these children originally were contacted via Internet chat rooms and other forms of electronic communication.

Moreover, little is known about the social and psychological profiles of online child victims and predators and the extent, if any, that they differ from offline victims and offenders? Online victims and pedophiles have accessibility to the Internet, and, thus, cyberstalkers may come from higher socioeconomic status groups than offline victims and child predators. In terms of offender characteristics, older pedophiles who have little experience on the Internet, may be less likely to engage in electronic stalking.

In response to proliferation of online stalkers, pedophiles, and other predators, a number of states in the U.S. have passed laws prohibiting online stalking and harassment (SafetyEd International Internet Safety organization, http://www.safetyed.org; Working to Halt Online Abuse, http://haltabuse.org/laws.html). Furthermore, existing laws, such as 18 U.S.C. Sec. 875c, have been used to apprehend those who use the Internet to transmit a threat to kidnap or harm another person across state or national borders (CyberSpace Law Center, http://cyber.lp.findlaw.com).

In 1994, the FBI began to take a proactive approach to online child predators and pornography after the alleged Internet-related abduction of 10-year-old Bruce Burdinski of Maryland (Kincaid, Salon.com, Aug. 24, 2000, pp. 1–5). Since the FBI established its Innocent Images sting operation in 1995, the Bureau reported that it has made 515 arrests, which resulted in 439 convictions (Kincaid, Salon.com, Aug. 24, 2000, pp. 1–5). The number of FBI sting operations have increased from 700 in 1998 to 1500 in 1999.

Other groups throughout the U.S. have organized to combat online stalking. The National Center for Missing and Exploited Children's CyberTipline had 1,848 tips about child enticement in a two-year period. On its web site, the SafetyEd International Internet Safety Organization reports that their experts have assisted in more than 700 cases of cyberstalking (SafetyEd International Internet Safety Organization, http://www.safetyed.org). A Chicago-based organization, the Chicago Child Advocacy Center, reported that 0.13% of its latest 4,000 child sex abuse cases was associated with electronic stalking.

Legislators, law enforcement agencies, and the courts also have focused their efforts in combating online pornography. Title V, known as the Communications Decency Act of 1996, of The Tele-communications Act of 1996, Pub. L. 104-110 Stat. 56, prohibited the electronic transmission of obscene or indecent communication and materials to persons under 18 years of age (Supreme Court of the United States, No. 96-511, http://www.ciec.org;http://thomas.loc.gov/cgi-bin/query). However, it was overturned by the U.S. Supreme Court. Other attempts to combat electronic pornography have had some successes. In September 1998, an international police operation arrested 107 people in eleven countries for their alleged involvement in the distribution of pornographic images of children (Richardson, Alex, ABCNEWS.com, Feb. 13, 2001). Seven men in the United Kingdom pled guilty to conspiracy to transmit indecent images of children via the Internet and were imprisoned for a combined total of 13 and 1/2 years.

Case Studies of Online Pedophiles

There have been a number of publicized cases of children who have been contacted by pedophiles and predators via the Internet. In 1999, a former vice president of Disney's Go Network, Patrick Naughton, was arrested for possession of child pornography, crossing state lines, and using the Internet in an effort to have sex with a young girl (Elder, Salon Media, Dec. 22, 1999, pp. 1–3). The 34-year-old suspect met the "fictional teenager," "krisLA" in a chat room known as "dads&daughterssex." She was actually an FBI agent who was part of a sting operation to catch online pedophiles. After meeting krisLA on the Internet, Mr. Naughton arranged to travel from Washington state to Santa Monica, California, where he was to meet her at the Santa Monica pier. The police arrested him as he attempted to initiate contact with the police decoy. At his trial, he was convicted of possession of child pornography, but the jury deadlocked on the charge of attempting to have sex with a minor. Mr. Naughton's defense was that he often spent time at online chat rooms, including "dads&daughterssex" and "girls&olderguys," because they were a source of fantasy for him. He chatted with krisLA to brag about his real-life accomplishments as a Disney executive and seek approval. When he met krisLA, he said that he assumed that she was of legal age.

There have been other cases of online predators and pedophiles being arrested (Chicago Tribune, July 6, 1997). In Massachusetts, 23-year-old John Rex, a resident of Chelmsford, was arrested and pled guilty to raping two boys whom he had met on the Internet. Mark Forston, a resident of Fresno, California, was convicted of sodomizing a child whom he had met on the web.

Community and Organizational Responses to Online Pedophiles

With the national concern over electronic pedophiles, community-based efforts have been undertaken to combat these criminal activities. Housewives, computer professionals, and others are volunteering their time to fight electronic child predators. Some of these volunteers noted evidence of child pornography being transmitted on the web and have taken a proactive approach to curbing this crime. Mrs. Nancy Casey, a 45-year-old mother of two children and a master seamstress, has gone undercover to hunt Internet pedophiles (Glod, Infowar.com, April 14, 2000, pp. 1–5). Mrs. Casey assists the police by posing as young girls at an Internet romance club. She posts messages from fictional characters who discuss their lives and problems, often telling sad stories about being an orphan or having parents who are in prison. Mrs. Casey reports that sexual predators respond to her messages quickly. As the Internet relationship develop, the cyberstalkers obtain further information about the girls and arrange for face-to-face meetings.

Mrs. Casey's undercover work has led to the arrest of several men, including suspected online child predator, Thomas Cook of Loudoun County (Glod, Infowar.com, April 14, 2000, pp. 1–5). Mr. Cook was arrested after contacting the fictional girl, Sabrina, a 15-year-old blonde, who went by the computer name, Satin Witch. Another suspect, Daniel Lunny, was arrested after responding to Mrs. Casey's fictional character, Noel, a 14-year-old girl who sang in her school chorus and described herself as a troublemaker. Mr. Lunny, who used the computer name, USA Man, reportedly told Noel that he really wanted to see her and not to tell her parents about their rendezvous. Another predator was arrested after responding to the fictional character, Angie, a school cheerleader who had just obtained her driver's license.

However, most online patrol organizations do not employ undercover strategies but encourage their members to contact the police when they have evidence of electronic criminal behavior. The Internet version of the Guardian Angels, Cyberangels, has 4000 members (www. cyberangels.org). Persons in this group monitor the web for sexual predators and pornography. Natasha Grigori, a computer technician in the Midwest, established an online patrol group which has 800 members (Glod, Infowar.com, April 14, 2000, pp. 1–5).

Law Enforcement Responses to Online Pedophiles

The lack of specific laws on electronic stalking is being remedied. In the past, anti-stalking laws did not specify electronic stalking. Currently, 26 online stalking and related laws have been enacted (National Conference of State Legislatures, http://www.ncsl.org). None of these laws deal exclusively with the electronic harassment of children by predators. Other laws allow a person to possess digitally-created pornographic images that contain no images of real children. Concerns about possible violations of the First Amendment can limit enforcement of these laws.

Law enforcement agencies' activities also have been hampered by a number of other obstacles. Due to identity-blocking software, they can have difficulty in tracing Internet pedophiles (Australian Broadcasting Corp., April 27, 2000, p. 2). Many police officers, prosecutors, and judges lack knowledge about online child predators and/or have insufficient funding, personnel, training, and policies and procedures for investigating complaints. Prosecution of suspects may be difficult or unlikely because of problems related to evidence and entrapment. Moreover, the adequacy of sentencing in these cases is uneven.

Cyberstalking and Adult Victims

Not only minors are being victimized via the Internet, but predators are using the web to stalk and harass adults. Sexual harassment via the Internet is another new concern, requiring new organizational responses. For example, the California Institute of Technology expelled a doctoral candidate for allegedly using e-mail to sexually harass another student (joc.mit.edu/cornell/latimes).

Besides facilitating person-to-person stalking, the Internet has made it easy for "hackers" to electronically stalk and harass organizations. These electronically knowledgeable individuals stalk organizations and hack into or penetrate their computer systems, destroying files, interfering with business activities, and sending destructive e-mail viruses. Furthermore, Internet service providers themselves can stalk individuals over the Internet through the use of so-called "cookies," electronic eavesdroppers that identify and monitor the recipient's electronic transmissions (Kelsey, Dick, Newsbytes.com, Jan. 27, 2000, pp. 1–2). As part of its $4 billion lawsuit against Yahoo, Universal Image charged the company with breaking Texas's anti-stalking statue by monitoring its computer clients without their permission. Yahoo was charged with sending cookies that invade their customers' hard drives without obtaining their prior permission.

Low cost, easy use, and anonymity are factors that facilitate cyberstalking and related criminal behaviors (NIJ, 1999, p. 1). Electronic stalkers may monitor communications at Internet chat rooms and send numerous threatening or obscene messages, called "flaming" the recipient, post malicious rumors about the target on electronic bulletin boards, and obtain private information about their potential victims. This anonymous, non-confrontational approach removes social disincentives for persons who otherwise would be hesitant about directly stalking their victims in face-to-face encounters or in telephone conversations. Stalkers also may invade the privacy of others by reading and/or tampering with a person's e-mail and/or computer system.

People might view online stalking of adults as harmless since computers can be turned at will. It is thought that one should not "surf the web" if she or he cannot cope with these events. Others see electronic stalking and harassment of adults as innocuous.

Furthermore, arresting and punishing cyberstalkers may violate a suspect's right to free speech under the First Amendment, the right to due process under the Fifth Amendment, and protection from unreasonable searches and seizures under the Fourth Amendment. In terms of free speech issues, where does one draw the line between stalking and free speech? Nevertheless, there is a belief that persistent electronic stalking and harassment frequently leads to offline violence against the victims and/or vandalism of their property (Godwin, M., Cyberstalking, www.investigative psych.com, pp. 1–2; Laughren, pp. 1–4).

Internet stalking, like offline stalking, centers around the issue of control and power. Online stalkers control their adult targets using different techniques. Online one can stalk and harass their targets by sending unsolicited e-mail of a hateful, obscene, and threatening nature, computer viruses, and junk e-mail. These types of e-mail communications appear to be the most prevalent form of cyberstalking and harassment. The online stalkers can use Usenet or other electronic news groups to post malicious rumors about their victim.

Prevalence of Electronic Stalking against Adults

Electronic stalking will increase in complexity and scope as more people use the Internet at home, in the workplace, and other settings (NIJ, 1999, p. 2). Internet service providers (ISP) report that they are getting an increased number of Internet stalking complaints (NIJ, 1999, p. 6). According to a 1999 NIJ report, one large ISP received a minimum of 15 Internet stalking complaints each month. One or two years earlier, the same ISP had received practically no complaints. A survey of Novell, Inc. employees in the United Kingdom revealed that 35% of the respondents reported being the victim of repeated unwelcome e-mails (Sanchez, Jana, IDG News Service/London Bureau, June 13, 1999, p. 1).

Various local law enforcement agencies, the FBI, and the U.S. Attorney's offices have received Internet stalking complaints (NIJ, 1999, p. 6). In Los Angeles, the District Attorney's Office estimates that 20% of the approximate 600 cases in its Stalking and Threat Assessment Unit involve Internet stalking. Likewise, in New York, the head of the Manhattan District Attorney's Office, Sex Crimes Unit estimates that 20% of its cases consist of Internet stalking. The New York Police Department's Computer Investigations and Technology Unit estimate that almost 40% of its cases consist of electronic harassment and threats, and these complaints have been made in the past three to four years. In their 3-year review, the National Criminal Intelligence Service (NCIS) in London found a dramatic increase in cyberstalking and other online crimes (Sanchez, Jana, IDG News Service/London Bureau, June 23, 1999). The NCIS reported that the threat of e-mail viruses has increased at annual rate of 49%.

Security firms also are seeing an increase in requests for combating electronic stalking. Park Dietz, president of Threat Assessment Group, Inc., in Newport Beach, CA, stated that his firm advises nearly 200 Fortune 500 firms about how to deal with online workplace stalking, harassment, and threats (Miller and Maharaj, Infowar.com, Jan. 27, 1999, pp. 1–3). Between 1994 and 1999, Dietz's firm has had thousands of cases of workplace harassment, stalking, and threats, and electronic stalking and harassment have increased from 0% to more than 25% in 1999. If stalking, harassment, and threats via pagers and faxes are included, the percentage increases to 50%.

College campuses are also targets for cyberstalking. A University of Cincinnati study of 4,446 randomly selected women in college found that 581 women (13%) were stalked, and 696 stalking incidents were reported. Twenty-five percent of these stalking incidents involved e-mail communications (NIJ, 1999, p. 7).

The prevalence of cyberstalking may vary depending on the setting. In contrast to other reports, the Stalking and Violence Project (SVP) found only 2% of stalking victims who had filed orders of protection had been e-mailed by their offenders.

The social profiles of electronic adult victims and perpetrators are relatively unknown. Nevertheless, some data suggest that like offline stalking, women are more likely to be victims of online stalking than men, and online stalkers are more likely to be male. There also is some evidence to suggest that adult victims and their stalkers, because of their access to the Internet, may be more likely to come from higher socioeconomic status groups than offline adult victims and perpetrators. With the expansion of free e-mail and Internet services, these differences probably will be reduced.

In addition, Godwin suggests that electronic stalkers vary in their propensity for violence (Godwin, www.investigative-psych.com). According to Godwin, there are two types of online stalkers: stranger and known stalkers. In online stranger stalking, neither the perpetrator nor the victim knows each other. In contrast, in online known stalking encounters, the perpetrators and targets frequently have developed casual or friendly relationships offline, and when their relationships deteriorate, they carry the conflict on to the Internet. Godwin suggests that online stranger stalkers are more likely to commit violence against their victims than non-stranger stalkers.

Case Studies of Adult Victims of Cyberstalking

There have been a number of publicized cases involving adult victims of electronic stalking. These incidents, which have occurred throughout the world, involve different types of Internet stalking and harassment. Targets have been both women and men who have been former dates, strangers, executives, and clients/customers. There was a reported case of online stalking involving members of a family. These stressful events frequently lead the victims to seek assistance from law enforcement, mental health professionals, and others.

Jayne Hitchcock, a resident of Maryland, became a victim of electronic stalking and harassment after submitting a manuscript to Woodside Literary Agency (Abuse of Usenet, Feb. 2001; Karl, 1999, pp. 1–2). Ms. Hitchcock became suspicious of the agency when it asked for $75 to read her submission, and she filed a complaint. Later, she discovered that a message had been posted on the World Wide Web, saying that she was available for sex anytime. Ms. Hitchcock reported that she received 25 to 30 telephone calls daily, with some calls coming from as far away as Germany.

Internet executives have been the victim of employment-associated cyberstalking. In 1996, Robert and Teresa Maynard, owners of a large Internet service provider, filed a temporary restraining order against an Internet stalker (The Dallas Morning News, 10-15-96). The suspect allegedly sent obscene e-mail communications to Mr. Maynard's wife. This escalated to threats of physical violence and included the information that the perpetrator knew where they lived. In addition to filing a restraining order, Mr. Maynard retained a security firm to guard his family.

In a case of employment-related Internet stalking, newspaper executives at the Lexington Herald Leader newspaper in Lexington, Kentucky, were stalked and harassed soon after a newspaper executive fired a freelance photographer for downloading pornography (CNN.COM, May 31, 2000). The female executive reported that she received phone calls from men who said they had met her in a chat room and wanted to meet her. She was inundated with items she had never ordered such as pornography and even received a supply of fish enough to stock a five-acre lake. A male executive at the newspaper received phone calls from women who said they had met him at a chat room that he had never visited. The publisher of the Knight-Ridder newspaper also received pornographic mail.

Another employment-related case of cyberstalking occurred in North Hollywood, California, where Doug Lantz's Internet business was allegedly attacked with threatening e-mail communications (ABCNEWS, May 1, 2000, pp. 1–2). One e-mail threatened to crush Mr. Lantz's skull, while another one warned the victim to close his business or it would be another nail in his coffin. The electronic stalker claimed to sleep only two hours a night and that his/her goal was to "get" the victim.

A University of Michigan student, Vincent A. Krause, reportedly was victimized when someone stalked him and hacked his computer password, and then used it to post racist jokes at a Usenet (Lester, 1998, pp. 1–2). The university reportedly received complaints from upset users, and a student group later marched on Mr. Krause's dorm room. Mr. Krause subsequently was exonerated of any wrongdoing.

Another University of Michigan student, Jake Baker, allegedly wrote a graphic fictional account of raping, torturing, and killing a woman and posted it on a computer bulletin board. The victim was given the name of one of Mr. Baker's classmates at the University of Michigan (United States of America v. Jake Baker and Arthur Gonda, U.S. District Court, Eastern District of Michigan, Southern Division). The case garnered public attention because the suspect used the real name of a student in his fictional work. In 1995, Mr. Baker, along with Arthur Gonda, were charged with interstate transmission of a threat.

Gary S. Dellapenta, a 50-year-old security guard in North Hollywood, was accused of electronic stalking, using the computer to commit fraud, deceive, or extort and solicitation to commit sexual assault on a woman (Miller, Greg & Maharaj, Davan, Infowar.com, January 27, 1999, pp. 1–3; Channel 3000, Jan. 22, 1999, pp. 1–2). Mr. Dellapenta allegedly stole a woman's identity, invaded her privacy, and posted a description of her on the Internet as a woman who fantasized about being raped (Channel, 3000, Jan. 22, 1999, pp. 1–2). The suspect also provided a description of what she looked like, her address, and how to bypass her home security procedures. Mr. Dellapenta initiated his electronic stalking and harassment when the woman rejected his romantic overtures.

In another case of alleged online stalking that resulted from rejected romantic overtures, Andy Archambeau was charged with violating Michigan's anti-stalking law for sending unwanted e-mail messages to a woman who had rejected him (Lester, High Technology Careers Magazine, 1998, pp. 1–2; Chicago Tribune, May 27, 1994). The 29-year-old graphic artist met his target using a video dating service. Mr. Archambeau continued to send e-mail communications, inviting her to meet in the Bahamas, even though the woman and police had told him to stop.

In Australia, a 22-year-old woman complained to the Queensland Police that she had received several unwanted and threatening e-mail communications (Australian Broadcasting Corp., April 27, 2000, pp. 1–2). She also complained to her Internet service provider who terminated the offender's account. The stalker then sent her a death threat using a different account.

The Chairwoman of the New South Wales Council on Violence Against Women reported that her daughter had received obscene communications on the Internet. Her daughter had used her own name while on the Internet, and this may have facilitated the transmission of these salacious materials.

One reported case of Internet stalking involved internal family matters in Emeryville, Ontario, Canada. A married couple reported that their home had been stalked by a mysterious, high-technology perpetrator, who apparently had tapped their phone lines and turned their power outlets off and on (The News-Times, April 18, 1997). The calls included burping and babbling sounds and assertions that the perpetrator had power to control appliances by remote control. Later, the couple's 15-year-old son confessed to being the cyberstalker (Legal Pad Times).

Persons in dating relationships and acquaintances, including co-workers, bosses, and those in current and past intimate relationships may be stalked online. The few persons in the SVP who reported being stalked via the Internet had been in current or past dating relationships. In SVP Case 478SF, Ms. A, who was in a lesbian relationship with Ms. B, received harassing e-mails at work from Ms. B. In SVP Case 468, Ms. C, who had been in a dating relationship with Mr. D, complained that Mr. D had invaded her privacy by reading her e-mail messages. The perpetrators in these cases used e-mails as part of a pattern of stalking and violence against their victims.

Psychological and Social Effects of Online Stalking

The psychological and social effects of electronic stalking, like offline forms of stalking, may be traumatic. Even though the victims may never see the perpetrator in the "real world," they can suffer intense emotional distress from the electronic stalking and because of the inability or reluctance of the police to arrest the online stalker. The victims worry that the electronic stalker will physically harm or kill them and their family and friends.

With the increase in the availability of information on the Internet, stalkers can gain access to the victims' credit card information and other personal information and can steal their credit cards and identities and illegally use their credit cards. Cyberstalking victims may find that their children and other family members are stalked and threatened by the perpetrators via e-mails, chat rooms, and electronic news groups.

The trauma of electronic stalking is exemplified in the case of the 28-year-old office worker who was stalked online by Gary Dellapenta (Miller & Maharaj, Infowar.com, Jan. 27, 1999, pp. 1–3). As a result of Mr. Dellapenta's Internet stalking and abuse, men would come to the victim's home in the middle of the night. The 28-year-old also received dozens of telephone calls from men who left obscene messages. The victim's mother reported that her daughter was so traumatized by Mr. Dellapenta that she lost her job, lost 35 pounds, and had significant difficulty getting out of bed in the morning. The victim lost her job at a real estate firm, in part, because the perpetrator had been making harassing calls at her job, and her job performance suffered as a consequence. She became so terrified of Mr. Dellapenta that she moved out of her home and resided with friends. The victim would not answer the phone and was fearful of going out of her new residence.

One female victim of online stalking, who met her perpetrator in an America Online chat room, was so fearful of her electronic stalker that she relocated to another city. The offender followed her in public and left her threatening messages, indicating that he knew her whereabouts. According to Donna Mason, executive director of Sacramento Area Stalking Survivors, being a stalking victim is like living in a glass house where the stalker is watching your every move and you do not know when the stalker will attack next.

Another online stalking victim, 31-year-old Jane Smith of Pennsylvania, was terrorized via e-mail by a man in Alaska, whom she had met in an Internet chat room (Woodall, Martha, www. standardtimes.com, April 1, 2000). Ms. Smith, who attended a conference on Internet stalking, reported that she had complained to the police and social service agencies, but they did not know how to handle her complaint. Since electronic stalking is so new, Ms. Smith indicated that she wants to form an organization to help other electronic victims.

Organizational Reactions to Internet Stalking

Media coverage of online stalking cases in recent years has encouraged the development of Internet stalking as a social problem (Lowney & Best, 1995, pp. 33–57). With the release of the National Institute of Justice (NIJ) report on cyberstalking on September 16, 1999, the Clinton Administration called for stricter laws against electronic stalking (Niccolai, IDG News Service/San Francisco Bureau, September 16, 1999). The NIJ Report recommended that states re-examine their own anti-stalking statutes to see if they cover electronic stalking and expand them if necessary. Some states have begun to modify their anti-stalking laws or use existing laws to fight electronic stalking. In addition, the NIJ Report called for stricter federal laws against threats delivered via electronic communications. The Justice Department and other law enforcement agencies have established programs to deal with the problems of Internet stalking and harassment.

Various Internet organizations, support groups, and victims advocacy organizations have been developed to assist the victims of Internet stalking and harassment and promote public awareness of this danger. The Internet itself abounds with a variety of web sites that describe the social, psychological, and legal aspects of Internet stalking and provide advice on how to cope with it. Internet organizations and groups, such as CyberAngels, Survivors of Stalking (SOS), and Web Police offer help to victims of online stalking and abuse (www.cyberangels.org; www.soshelp.org; www.Web-Police.org).

New technological innovations and procedures are being developed to prevent or minimize such abuse. Predators and the proliferation of pornographic materials led to the development of screening devices for computers. Furthermore, threats to computer security and personal privacy have increased the use of anonymous re-mailers, secret passwords, and encryption technology to protect the privacy of computer users. Paradoxically, these technological innovations also can be used by predators to carry out their stalking activities.

Cyberstalking cases can have relevance to civil rights law under the First, Fourth, and Fifth Amendments (ICLU – Your Rights in Cyberspace, http://www. Law.indiana.edu; http://www.vtw.org; www.law.ucla.edu; www.gseis.ucla.edu). Defenders of the First Amendment argue that there can be a fine line between the offender's stalking and harassing activities on the one hand, and their constitutional right to free speech (Watts v. United States, 394 U.S. 705 1969). There is frequently a conflict between promoting a stalking suspect's right to free speech and due process under the Fifth Amendment and protecting Internet stalking victims from further harm. Likewise, there are similar conflicts between protecting victims and yet ensuring a stalking suspect's protection against unreasonable searches and seizures of computer-related hardware and software under the Fourth Amendment. Another interesting organizational response to the growth of the Internet is

the emergence of the online pedophile groups, which provide support and resources for child predators to gratify their fantasies
online.

Another natural outgrowth of organizational responses to
online stalking is the new emphasis on public education and computer civility. Critics point out that the elementary and secondary
schools and colleges are teaching students how to use the Internet,
but do not teach them cyber ethics (CNN.com, 2000, pp. 1–2). There
is concern that many individuals, especially young people, do
not see online stalking, hacking, and intellectual property right violations as illegal. These types of crimes are not seen as illicit
because they occur outside the view of other people. Educational
conferences and behavioral sciences research are adding to new
knowledge about stalking. For example, a conference at the
University of Pennsylvania School of Nursing on March 31, 2000,
discussed how the Internet was changing the ways law enforcement and the courts combat stalking (Woodall, Martha, www.
standardtimes.com, April 1, 2000).

Conclusion

This analysis has described the role of online technology in
facilitating stalking behaviors. Technology now enables individuals and organizations to achieve their goals through cyberstalking.
With the expansion of the web, existing anti-stalking laws have
been modified or new laws have been passed to cope with online
stalking. The courts, law enforcement, civil rights groups, and
other organizations develop solutions to perplexing issues, such as
how to protect children and adults from online stalking while pre-
serving people's rights to free speech and privacy and the suspects'
rights to due process and freedom from unreasonable searches and
seizures. Research is needed to determine the prevalence and social
patterns of online stalking, its sequelae, and the impact of law
enforcement efforts on online stalking and the preservation of civil
liberties.

3

Characteristics of Stalking Victims and Offenders

The previous chapters found that stalking frequently occurs in different types of social relationships, and these relationships may influence how offenders use stalking to control, harass, and retaliate against their victims. To better understand stalking as a form of control and intimidation, it is helpful to assess the social characteristics of victims and perpetrators.

Little is known about the social attributes of stalkers and their victims, in part, because of the difficulties inherent in studying stalking in the general population. Most of the investigations to date have employed small forensic and clinical samples, which primarily have been self-selected samples of convenience (Dietz, et al., 1991; Hall, 1998; Harmon, Rosner, & Owens, 1995; Meloy, 1996; Meloy & Gothard, 1995; Raskin & Sullivan, 1974; Schwartz-Watts & Morgan, 1998; Zona, Sharma, & Lane, 1993). Their subjects have included erotomanics and others with psychiatric diagnoses.

The present analysis focuses on cases of stalking which seldom come to the attention of psychiatrists. In these cases, the stalking tends to be initiated when relationships have become conflict-oriented. Persons may stalk their targets to control, terrorize, or retaliate against them for some perceived mistreatment. Stalking may occur when persons try to terminate or actually end a relationship. The stalking transpires before, during, and after a relationship.

It is important to note that these behaviors take place in a wide range of relationships that involve family members, relatives, individuals in dating relationships, acquaintances, and even strangers. Zona, et al. (1993) categorized stalkers in relationships as simple obsessional followers.

One of the central issues in the present analysis is whether the social characteristics of stalkers and their targets are patterned and reflective of power differences and social dynamics among different social groups. Is a person's age predictive of stalking? Does the victim's gender influence the type of stalking behaviors? These types of questions will help to determine if profiles of perpetrators and victims can be constructed. Moreover, they allow for further exploration into the dynamics underlying stalker/victim interactions and the victimization experience.

Gender of Victims and Stalkers

According to the National Violence Against Women (NVAW) survey, women are the primary victims of stalking, and men are the main offenders (NIJ, 1998, p. 10). Seventy-eight percent of the self-reported stalking victims in the NVAW study were women and 22% were men. Similar findings were obtained in the Stalking & Violence Project (SVP) study (Morewitz, 2000a; Morewitz, 2000b). Based on a random sample of 519 orders of protection, 78% of the targets in the SVP study were women and 22% were men (See Appendix B). In a study of college students on one campus, 35% of the women and 18% of the men surveyed reported having been stalked (Fremouw, Westrup & Pennypacker, 1997).

Various investigations have found stalking in both heterosexual and homosexual/lesbian relationships, with the heterosexual form to be the most prevalent (NIJ, 1998, p. 10; Pathe and Mullen, 1994; Fremouw, Westrup & Pennypacker, 1997). The NVAW authors reported that 94% of the offenders identified by female victims and 60% of the stalkers identified by male victims were male (NIJ, 1998, p. 10). In the SVP, 95% of pursuers reported by female victims, and 23% of the offenders reported by male victims were male.

In male-to-female stalking, men use stalking to control, punish, and instill fear in the women. Men employ stalking along with repeated threats, harassing behaviors, physical violence, and vandalism to achieve these goals. For example, in SVP Case 351, Mr. A, a 34-year-old single man, used stalking to control and punish Ms. B, who previously had been in a dating relationship with him. Ms. B charged that Mr. A had been stalking her on a regular basis. Once, while allegedly under the influence of illicit drugs and alcohol, the perpetrator approached Ms. B on the street and told her to relocate in two weeks or suffer the consequences.

Seventy-seven percent of the male victims in the SVP reported being stalked by female perpetrators. As in the case of male-to-female stalking, women employ stalking to control, retaliate, and terrorize their victims. SVP Case 94 C shows how a woman, Ms. C, engaged in stalking and other forms of abuse to retaliate against Mr. D, a 30-year-old single man whom she had been dating. Mr. D claimed that Ms. C had harassed and threatened him. She had broken his car window, created a disturbance at his residence, and threatened him with physical harm. The distress caused by her pursuit and harassment had forced him to take time off from his employment as a bus driver.

Few male stalking victims in the SVP identified other males as stalkers. Men in various types of relationships are less likely to be pursued by men than by women perhaps because of social norms. Another factor may be that male stalking victims are less likely to request orders of protection and/or report being pursued by male than female victims. Also, men may not perceive such behaviors as stalking or may be too embarrassed to report it. However, the small percentage of male victims in the SVP makes it difficult to generalize these results.

Victims Know Their Offenders

The NVAW results confirm previous reports that most victims are acquainted with their stalkers (NIJ, 1998, p. 10). Only 23% of female victims and 36% of male victims were followed by strangers. Thirty-eight percent of female victims were stalked by current or former husbands (NIJ, 1998, p. 11). Ten percent of female stalking victims in a current or past lesbian relationship reported being pursued by their partners. Fourteen percent of the female stalking victims in the NVAW study were followed by current or former dates and boyfriends (NIJ, 1998, p. 11).

In the SVP, all of the victims knew their offenders (Morewitz, 2000a; Morewitz, 2000b). A lower percent of women (27%) were pursued by current husbands in the SVP than in the NVAW report. About the same percentage of female stalking victims (12%) in the SVP reported being followed by a current or past cohabiting partner as those in the NVAW report. Female stalking victims in the SVP had twice the rate of being stalked by current or former dates or boyfriends (36%) than female victims in the NVAW survey.

Male victims in the NVAW investigation tended to be stalked by strangers and acquaintances, 90% of whom were male (NIJ, 1998, p. 11). Thirty-four percent of male stalking victims were followed by acquaintances and 36% of male stalking victims were stalked by strangers. It was not evident why male victims were stalked by male acquaintances and strangers. The authors indicate that homosexual men have a higher chance of being stalked than heterosexual men. They found that men who had ever cohabited with other men or had ever lived in gay relationships were at greater risk of being stalked than men who had not. These results are consistent with the literature that shows that homosexuals in intimate relationships can face physical and emotional forms of abuse (Island & Letellier, 1991; Healey & Smith, 1998). In some instances, male-to-male stalking of strangers and acquaintances may be due to homophobia or the desire to initiate new intimate relations (NIJ, 1998, p. 12). In other situations, the pursuit of males may be associated with gang conflicts.

There were only four cases of acquaintance harassment in the SVP. In SVP Cases 10C (male offender and male victim) and 186C (female offender and female victim), the offenders engaged in a variety of stalking behaviors. However, neither of the two victims perceived the offenders' behaviors as stalking.

In the SVP, 35% of the male victims were stalked by females in current or former dating relationships, and 20% were followed by their current spouses (Morewitz, 2000a; Morewitz, 2000b). There were only six SVP cases in which male targets reported that they were stalked by males. This represent 23% of all the SVP cases in which men were followed. Five of the six male-to-male cases involved male victims who formerly had dated and lived with the male offenders. The last case of male-to-male case consisted of a male child who was stalking his stepfather.

The five SVP male partner cases support the NVAW's hypothesis that men who have cohabited with other men are at increased risk of being pursued by their male roommates or partners. In SVP Case 506SF, Mr. E, a single man, stated that Mr. F, a 30-year-old man whom he had lived with, had stalked, assaulted, and harassed him after their gay lover relationship ended. One day the offender stepped on the victim's left foot, causing a knee injury, which later necessitated medical treatment. The next day when the perpetrator parked outside his residence, Mr. E filed a police report.

In the four other SVP male partner cases, the male victims did not indicate that they had any homosexual relationship with the offenders. However, in SVP Case 500SF, Mr. G, a single man, charged that Mr. H, a 28-year-old man whom he had resided with, had threatened to humiliate him by sending letters and photographs to his family and employer. This threat may have been based on evidence of a previous homosexual relationship, and the disclosure of this fact would be detrimental to Mr. G. In addition to making threats, the offender attempted to rape Mr. G, and hit him multiple times. He also physically restrained him, stalked him on his way to work, and left 25 messages on his answering machine during one day.

Pathe and Mullen (1997) reported 10 cases of female-to-female stalking. It is interesting to note that the NVAW did not report on female-to-female stalking. Their exclusion of data on female-to-female stalking is surprising since studies have shown that lesbians face a variety of abuses in their relationships. For example, Lie and Gentlewarrior (1991) found that more than 50% of the 1,099 lesbians surveyed indicated that they had been abused by a lesbian partner.

There were six cases of women who reported being stalked by other women in the SVP. Three of the cases consisted of female victims who had been in dating relationships with other women. One case involved a woman who had been stalked by her female roommate and business partner. The two women jointly owned a residence. The two remaining cases involved relationships with relatives.

In SVP Case 478SF, Ms. I had been stalked, assaulted, and harassed by Ms. J, a 32-year-old single woman, after the breakup of their year-long dating relationship. Ms. I had met Ms J. through a lesbian personal advertisement. She accused the offender of stalking and ambushing her in a locker room. Ms. J had thrown a chalk block at her head, threatened her with physical harm, and had driven dangerously with her in the car. The perpetrator repeatedly harassed the victim and her friends by telephone and had e-mailed her at work. In addition, Ms. J had threatened to commit suicide if Ms. I did not return to her. Ms. I noted that during their relationship, the perpetrator used strict rules to control her contacts with other people.

Gender and Type of Stalking Behaviors

Differences in the type of stalking behaviors may be related to the gender of the stalking victims. In the NVAW survey, female victims were more likely than male victims to indicate that the offenders followed them, spied on them, waited outside their home or work, and made unwelcome phone calls (NIJ, 1998, p. 12). About an equal proportion of male and female stalking victims indicated that the perpetrators sent unwanted letters or items, vandalized their property, or killed/threatened their pets (NIJ, 1998, p. 12).

In contrast, the SVP found that gender was related to only one form of stalking behavior. Male stalking victims were more likely than female stalking victims to report that their property had been vandalized. However, the small percentage of male victims in the SVP makes it difficult to generalize from these results.

Age of Stalking Victims and Stalkers

Younger adults, ages 18–29, are more likely to be stalked than older adults (NIJ, 1998, p. 10). In addition, cases of adolescent obsessional following have been identified (McCann, 1998). In the NVAW, 52% of stalking victims were between 18 and 29 years of age and 22% were in the 30–39 age group when the stalking began (NIJ, 1998, p. 10). Fremouw, et al. (1997), in their survey of college students on one campus, found that about 35% of the women and 18% of the men surveyed reported being stalked. Cupach and Spitzberg (1998) found substantial evidence of stalking or "obsessive relational intrusion" among undergraduate men and women at three colleges.

The age of offenders is less certain. The NVAW investigation did not include findings on the age of perpetrators. Zona, et al. (1993) reported that the average age of their erotomanic and obsessional subjects was 35. The age trends among stalkers in the general population has not been documented. Because stalking frequently occurs in intimate or dating relationships and these relationships often involve persons of similar ages, it is expected that offender age will parallel victim age.

In the SVP, 73% of the stalkers were between 18 and 40 years of age. Fourteen percent were in the 18–25 age group, 59% were in the 26–40, 26% were in the 41–60 age group, and 1% were 60 years of age and older. This age distribution was similar to the age distribution of offenders accused of all forms of domestic violence.

Maturation Hypothesis

The age of offenders in the SVP suggest that there may be a maturation process among stalkers. Persons who are older than 40 years of age are less likely to stalk than those under 40. These results parallel criminological research that shows that middle aged persons mature out of violent criminal career patterns (Warr, 1998; Sampson & Laub, 1993; Elliott, 1994). However, the SVP findings differ from criminological reports that show violent criminal offenses peak around the age of 19. In the SVP, a majority of the stalkers are in the 26–40 age group. Caution should be taken in comparing stalking to violent criminal offenses since the former encompasses a variety of criminal and non-criminal conduct, whereas the latter involves exclusively on criminal behaviors.

Additional evidence of the maturation hypothesis can be tested by analyzing the extent to which stalking and physical violence varied among offenders of different age groups. In the SVP, the maturation hypothesis was accepted since stalking was positively related to violence against persons in the youngest age groups, 18–25 and 26–40, but not in the 41–60 age group. In fact, there were an insufficient number of offenders in the over 60 age group to even include this group in the analysis. Among offenders, ages 18–25, stalking was positively related to two violent acts against persons: choking and pushing the victims. Perpetrators in the 26–40 age group who used more "close-up" forms of stalking, e.g., came to the victim's home, were more likely to assault their victims. In contrast, stalking by offenders, ages 41–60, was not related to violence.

SVP Case 143 offers an example of a young offender, Mr. O, a 23-year-old man, who repeatedly stalked and threatened his wife, Mrs. P. She accused her husband, who was living apart from her, of coming to her home to remove his belongings and threatening to "blow up" her house and car. Mr. O also pushed his wife's head through a wall and has hit her. He also threatened to come back to her home with his "boys." Mr. O reportedly drives past her house on a daily basis. The offender has threatened to cut the victim's car brake line as a Christmas gift and break into her house.

With regard to committing vandalism against the victim's property, the maturation hypothesis also was supported. Stalking was positively associated with vandalizing the victim's property among offenders in the 18–25 age group, but not among offenders in the two older age groups.

Ethnic/Racial Background of Victims and Offenders

Are there ethnic/racial differences among stalking victims? If yes, what are the implications for understanding the social patterns of stalking and power dynamics of ethnic/racial groups? The NVAW survey found that when comparing White women with non-White women, there were no differences in stalking victimization during their lifetime (NIJ, 1998, p. 8). Both White and non-White women had a lifetime rate of 8.2%.

The NVAW also analyzed the lifetime rate of stalking victimization for women in separate ethnic/racial groups. American Indian/ Alaska Native women reported twice the rate than women of other racial and ethnic groups (NIJ, 1998, p. 8). These results are consistent with the evidence in the literature that Native Americans have a higher violence rate than other women (NIJ, 1998, p. 9). Nevertheless, these findings should be viewed with caution given the few number of American Indians/Alaska Native groups studied.

Asian-American and Pacific Islander women in the NVAW investigation were less likely to be stalked than women in other racial and ethnic groups (NIJ, 1998, p. 9). The small number of women in these groups makes it difficult to draw conclusions. It may be that the cultural values of the importance of close family ties and harmony may inhibit Asian women from reporting physical and emotional abuse. However, Yoshihama and Sorenson (1994)'s study of spousal abuse in Japan does not support this hypothesis. Also, there may be differences between Asian and Pacific Islander women that cannot be ascertained since stalking data on these two groups were combined in the NVAW project.

For male stalking victims in the NVAW study, no significant differences in lifetime stalking rates were found among different ethnic/racial groups. However, the small number of male stalking victims studied makes it difficult to generalize. In regard to persons of Hispanic and non-Hispanic origin, the NVAW project found no significant differences in lifetime stalking victimization among males and females of Hispanic and non-Hispanic origin.

The NVAW survey did not report the ethnic and racial backgrounds of followers. Since stalking occurs in intimate and dating relationships and these relationships often involve persons of similar ethnic/racial backgrounds, we would expect stalkers and targets to have similar ethnic and racial backgrounds. Nevertheless, many intimate and dating relationships involve persons from different ethnic and racial groups, making it difficult to ascertain the ethnic/racial trends among stalkers. Moreover, there will be limited ethnic/racial data on offenders who are strangers or acquaintances.

The SVP found that the ethnic status of the stalkers was similar to that of all persons accused of different forms of domestic violence including stalking (Morewitz, 2000a; Morewitz, 2000b). Fifty-one percent of the stalkers in the SVP were African-American, 25% White, and 19% Hispanic. For offenders accused of all types of domestic violence, 53% were African-American, 21% were White, and 20% Hispanic.

Ethnic Factors in Stalking and Violence

An important research issue is whether ethnic factors are related to stalking and violence. This topic parallels research on the role of ethnic factors in facilitating domestic abuse. For example, the National Crime Victimization Survey found that African-American females had the highest rate of abuse by intimate partners than any other ethnic/racial group for the 1993–1998 period (US Department of Justice, www.ojp.usdoj.gov/bjs). In regard to stalking, the cultural emphasis on male authority and aggression and female subordination and stoicism may foster stalking in certain ethnic groups (Fernandez-Esquer & McCloskey, 1999). In contrast, other ethnic groups may not have cultural traditions and family structure that promote stalking.

It is helpful to draw upon Markowitz and Felson (1998)'s attitude mediation hypothesis to explain the relationship between social characteristics such as offender ethnicity and following. They suggest that young people hold positive attitudes towards demonstrating courage, seeking retribution, and being antagonistic. Persons with these attitudes have a greater chance of engaging in violent crimes than those who do not hold these attitudes. In terms of stalking, persons in certain groups may hold similar attitudes that encourage stalking.

According to the SVP results, the relationship between following and violence varied significantly among Hispanic, White, and African-American offenders (Morewitz, 2000a; Morewitz, 2000b). Among Hispanic perpetrators, stalking was positively associated with throwing the victim down. For Hispanic offenders living in census tracts with a median income between $20,000 and $39,999, stalking also was positively related to choking the victims.

Among African-American and White perpetrators, stalking was not related to physical violence against the victims.

In the SVP, stalking was positively associated with vandalism among White and African-American perpetrators but not among Hispanic offenders (Morewitz, 2000a; Morewitz, 2000b). For instance, SVP Case 405C offers evidence of a White offender, Mr. W, a 29-year-old male, who reportedly stalked, harassed, and vandalized the property of Ms. X, whom he had dated and lived with previously. One day, the perpetrator broke into the victim's apartment and lit all of her candles. He waited there with the lights off until she arrived home.

Socioeconomic Status of Stalking Victims and Offenders

Determining the socioeconomic status of victims and offenders is especially problematic because of the difficulties in collecting data on the occupation, income, and educational level of the victims and pursuers. Traditionally, clinical and forensic studies have found that obsessional followers frequently come from middle-income groups (Harmon, Rosner, & Owens, 1995; Meloy & Gothard, 1995). There is also clinical and forensic evidence that women in low-socioeconomic status groups tend to stalk men and women of higher socioeconomic status (Harmon, Rosner, & Owens, 1995). There are insufficient data to generalize these small clinical and forensic reports to the general population.

The NVAW study did not report on the socioeconomic status of either the stalking victims or offenders. In the SVP, a variety of census tract-based socioeconomic status data were obtained for each stalker and victim. Using the last known address of the stalkers and victims, census-tract level median income data and other socioeconomic status variables were analyzed. The majority of the stalking victims and offenders lived in census tracts with a median income of less than $40,000. Forty-five percent of the followers resided in census tracts with a median income of less than $20,000. Fifty percent lived in census tracts with a median income between $20,000 and $39,999. Only 5% of the stalkers in the SVP lived in census tracts with a median income between $40,000 and $59,999.

These data were similar to that of offenders in the SVP who had been accused of all forms of domestic violence including stalking. Forty percent of those accused of all types of domestic abuse lived in census tracts with a median income of less than $20,000 and 52% resided in census tracts between $20,000 and $39,999. Only 7% lived in census tracts with a median income in the range of $40,000 and $59,999, and 1% resided in census tracts with a median income between $60,000 and $79,999.

Conclusion

This chapter has shown that the social characteristics of stalkers and their victims are patterned and fairly well predictable. For instance, the male-to-female form of stalking is the most prevalent type. These social characteristics reflect the social and psychological dynamics among social groups and in society. In the case of male-to-female stalking, male dominance and female submission to power differentials underlie much of the social dynamics in these interactions.

Another important point is that the social characteristics of stalkers and their victims actually may influence the nature of stalking in different relationships. For instance, younger aged stalkers may be more likely than older aged stalkers to commit both stalking and violent offenses. Persons in various social groups may hold attitudes that facilitate or inhibit stalking. Thus, younger aged stalkers may feel the need to be aggressive and combative, and these attitudes encourage both stalking and physical violence. Future research needs to determine the extent to which the attitudes of stalkers and victims affect the nature and prevalence of stalking.

An analysis of the social characteristics of pursuers and victims also illustrates the possible role of life course changes in fostering or blocking stalking in relationships. As people age and move in and out of relationships, their tendency to engage in stalking behaviors may change as well. Various social, psychological, and physical conditions may foster the onset and course of stalking. Persons over 60 years of age may be less likely to stalk their targets and commit violence because of their limited physical condition and or greater life experiences, while those in the 18–29 age group (or younger) have the physical endurance and attitudinal readiness to stalk and assault their victims.

Moreover, stalkers and their victims are influenced by societal stereotypes and expectations concerning their roles in different relationships. For instance, in many cultures, men are expected to be aggressive and pursue their targets in dating relationships, and women are supposed to be passive, yet "play hard to get." Additional research is necessary to assess what part societal expectations play in determining the characteristics of stalking relationships.

Finally, to what degree does social change affect the social characteristics of stalkers and victims? For example, as women gain more power, status, and economic resources in the workplace, will there be an increased rate of female-to-male forms of stalking? Likewise, as the socioeconomic status of other social groups changes, will there be changes in the stalking rates and characteristics of these groups?

4

The Impact of Stalking

Studies show that stalking is psychological terrorism (Hall, 1998, p. 133). Victims fear that their stalker will injure or murder them and their family and friends (National Violence Against Women— NVAW survey, NIJ, 1998, p. 13). These fears are supported by the fact that stalkers do resort to physical violence, especially among persons in relationships (Cupach & Spitzberg, 1998). Friends, family members, and even bystanders who try to protect the victim may be attacked by the stalker, and these third parties can be traumatized.

Caught in the Stalker's Prison

Stalking is especially stressful because it makes the victims feel like they are living under the stalker's control and are powerless to escape (Morewitz, 2001c). Stalkers loiter outside the victims' homes and/or work places and harass them by phone, e-mail, and fax. Victims feel as if they are living in a prison of the stalkers' making and curtail their usual activities to avoid the stalkers.

Stalking and Violence Project (SVP) Case 52C illustrates the powerlessness of Ms. A, who had been stalked and threatened by Mr. B, whom she had been dating (See Appendix B). The perpetrator repeatedly tried to get the victim to resume the relationship. One day, the offender tried to force his way into Ms. A's home, threatening to cut her throat and kill anyone who was with her.

Ms. A believes that one day Mr. B will make good on his threats. She is very frightened and tired of being in "his prison." Her feelings of powerlessness are worsened by the fact that when she calls the police, the perpetrator vanishes and returns to continue the harassment.

Coping with the Uncertainty of Stalking

Stalking can be especially stressful if the victim is unsure about what the stalker will do next. Victims frequently worry that the offender will harm them and their family. Their fears are compounded by the fact that the perpetrators ignore orders of protection and attempt to bypass other measures for stopping the stalking. In SVP Case 101C, Ms. C, a graduate student, briefly had dated Mr. D, another graduate student. He stalked and harassed her for three years. After one year of stalking and harassment, Ms. C complained to the university's dean, who arranged for a no-contact agreement between the two individuals; it did not work. Her victimization continued for a third year with the offender's attempt to run over the victim with his truck. Ms. C was afraid for her life and distressed that the university's intervention had been ineffective.

Dealing with the Stalker's Bizarre Behavior

Certain stalkers who may be suffering from severe psychological problems engage in a variety of bizarre and erratic behaviors that can create significant stress and anxiety for the victims.

SVP Case 18C illustrates the bizarre actions of a stalker. Mrs. G claimed that her husband, Mr. H, stalked and threatened to kill her. He repeatedly talked about dying together, and even took out an life insurance policy on her. He said that "We are going to die soon, and we should die happy." The perpetrator planned to kill her and then shoot at the police, who would, in turn, kill him. Mr. H sneaked up on his wife from behind while barefoot, stole her jewelry and pawned it, and disappeared for days at a time. As a result of these bizarre behaviors, Mrs. G is very frightened and anxious and sleeps with weapons for protection.

Physical Trauma

Stalking survivors frequently sustain physical trauma from stalker attacks. In the SVP, a majority of the stalking victims (70%) reported that they had suffered physical injuries at the hands of their offenders. Thirteen percent indicated that they had sought medical attention for their injuries.

SVP Case 379C illustrates the physical trauma sustained by stalking victims. In this case, Ms. E had been stalked by Mr. F. He repeatedly punched her in the head and held her in a headlock. Ms. E sustained bruises and bumps from being assaulted and felt very intimidated.

Emotional Trauma

The severe stressors associated with stalking and threats can lead to a significant decline in the physical and emotional health of the survivors and their family members (Pathe & Mullen, 1997, p. 14; Roberts & Dziegielewski, 1996; Cupach & Spitzberg, 1998, pp. 252–253).

Roberts and Dziegielewski (1996) suggest that depression, suicide, and anxiety can result from stalking victimization. Even years after the stalking has ended, survivors may be fearful that the stalking may resume at any time (Hall, 1998, p. 135). In Pathe and Mullen (1997)'s study, 75% of the victims had intense feelings of powerlessness, and 24% even had thought about committing suicide. Eighty-three percent reported experiencing increased anxiety, including jumpiness, the shakes, panic attacks, excessive vigilance, and exaggerated startle response. One stalking survivor developed stress-related dental problems, which required dental work and wearing a mouth guard at night (Pathe & Mullen, 1997, p. 14).

Seventy-four percent of the stalking survivors stated that they suffered from sleep disturbance caused by persistent nightmares or repeated phone calls by the pursuer (Pathe & Mullen, 1997, p. 14). Forty-eight percent of the victims had an appetite disturbance, and 43% noted that they had fluctuations in their weight. Some victims gained weight in order to reduce their attractiveness to the pursuer, but they were generally unsuccessful in warding off the offenders.

Thirty percent of the survivors stated that they had suffered from persistent nausea. One female target felt the urge to vomit every time she came to work because the stalker waited for her there. Twenty-seven percent of the survivors complained of indigestion, and 23% had a change in their bowel habits.

Targets in the SVP reported a variety of stress-related symptoms from the stalking and harassment. In SVP Case 80C, Mrs. L reported having constant headaches and high blood pressure because of the emotional stresses of being victimized by her husband, Mr. M. In SVP Case 18C, Mrs. G was frightened and nervous because of her husband's death threats and stalking behaviors.

Alcohol use and smoking increased as a result of the stalking victimization for 23% of the survivors surveyed in Pathe and Mullen's study (Pathe & Mullen, 1997, p. 14). Pathe and Mullen noted that 55% of the survivors reported excessive tiredness or weakness as a long standing health problem. Forty-seven percent of the survivors had difficulties because of increased frequency and severity of headaches.

Stalking victims report the development of new problems or a worsening of current health problems, such as asthma and psoriasis due to their stalking victimization (Pathe & Mullen, 1997, p. 14).

Stalking survivors may develop the symptoms of Post Traumatic Stress Disorder (PTSD), an anxiety disorder resulting from exposure to a traumatic event or situation (Roberts & Dziegielewski, 1996; Wallace & Silverman, 1996; Pathe & Mullen, 1997). Symptoms of PTSD include recurrent nightmares, decreased responsiveness to the external world, exaggerated startle response, irritability, anxiety, and depression.

In Pathe and Mullen (1997)'s investigation, 37% of the stalking victims met the criteria for having a diagnosis of PTSD. Fifty-five percent of the stalking survivors in their study had intrusive recollections and flashbacks of their stalking experiences. The ringing of a telephone or a knock at the door triggered these reactions in several victims. In some cases, stalking victims have had these intrusive recollections and flashbacks many years after the stalking ordeal had ended. Victims had flashbacks when they saw people or items that triggered the memory of the harassment. One victim reported that she becomes distressed when she sees the make and model of the car driven by her pursuer. Thirty-eight percent of the victims had numbing or avoidance responses, especially detachment and estrangement from people (Pathe & Mullen, 1997, p. 14).

Personality changes have been reported (Hall, 1998, p. 134). Hall (1998) found that 88% of the stalking victims had become cautious, 41% frequently felt paranoid, 52% were frightened easily, and 27% showed more aggression since the stalking began (Hall, 1998, p. 134). Female victims reported that they were less trusting, particularly of men, were more suspicious, and more isolated from others since the stalking was initiated (Hall, 1998, p. 134). Stalking survivors also suffer from lower self-image in response to stalking (Robert & Dziegielewski, 1996). Their lowered self-image may result from their feelings of powerlessness in dealing with the stalker and guilt feelings that they are somehow to blame for causing the stalking.

Disrupted Family/Social Functioning

Impaired social, family, occupational, and educational functioning have been reported by stalking survivors (Hall, 1998, pp. 133–135; Pathe & Mullen, 1997, p. 14). Thirty-nine percent of the survivors in Pathe and Mullen (1997)'s study changed their homes (some up to five times), seven percent relocated to another state, and three percent went abroad. The family, friends, and acquaintances of the victims can have their lives severely disrupted (Pathe & Mullen, 1997, p. 14).

The family members of stalking survivors also can suffer the same types of stress-related symptoms as the primary stalking victim. In SVP Case 399C, Mrs. R's eldest daughter had trouble sleeping and was uneasy and edgy because of her father's stalking and harassment of her mother.

SVP Case 399C provides an example in which an offender's stalking and threatening behaviors can isolate the victim from her family and friends. Mrs. U stated that her husband, Mr. V, is very jealous and refused to allow her to see her family and friends. Furthermore, Mr. V has threatened that if she ever left him, he would hurt her seriously and kidnap their daughters and take them to Mexico.

Adverse Impact at the Workplace and School

Offenders may stalk and harass targets at their work place and threaten the victim's supervisors and co-workers. The stalkers may contact the victim's supervisor in order to get the victim in trouble or fired. This behavior may have an intimidating effect on the supervisor.

In SVP Case 509SF, Mr. W, who was a relative of Ms. V, had received death threats and had been stalked at work by Ms. V. The stalking target complained that Ms. V had gone to his work place and showed his supervisor a restraining order against him in order to get him fired.

Victims may be fired, transferred, or lose time from work because of stalking (Pathe & Mullen, 1997, p. 14; NIJ, 1998, pp. 20–21). Some stalking survivors quit their jobs and some change residences, leaving their family and friends (NIJ, 1998, pp. 20–21; Hall, 1998, pp. 133–135; Pathe & Mullen, 1997, p. 14). Thirty-seven percent of the victims in Pathe and Mullen (1997)'s investigation had to change their jobs, schools, or careers in response to the stalking (Pathe & Mullen, 1997, p. 14).

The targets of stalking take off time from work or school to obtain legal protection, change residences, or use other strategies to stop the stalking. According to the NVAW survey, 26% of the stalking targets had lost time from work because of their victimization (NIJ, 1998, pp. 20–21). Seven percent of these victims stated that they never returned to work. Pathe and Mullen (1997) reported that 53% of the victims had a decrease or loss in attendance at work or school (Pathe & Mullen, 1997, p. 14). Not surprisingly, victims report a loss of income as a result of the stalking victimization.

In SVP Case 237C, Mrs. Y complained that her husband, Mr. Z, previously had stalked her, punched her in the face, and stole over $10,000 of her money. Now she was unable to work because she was afraid that her husband would take all of her money and property and hurt her and her children.

The psychological terror caused by the stalking leads to diminished concentration and productivity on the job and may make victims afraid to go to work. In SVP Case 406C, Mrs. A stated that after her husband, Mr. B, assaulted her and threatened to kill her, she was so scared and anxious that she could not concentrate at work.

Workplace stalking can make the targets feel afraid and ashamed to go to work. SVP Case 33C illustrates the trauma and stigma of workplace stalking. Ms. C, who had lived with Mr. D, complained that Mr. D had telephoned and e-mailed her at work with threatening messages and had called her supervisor in an attempt to have her fired. Subsequently, Ms. C became fearful and ashamed to go to work.

Conditions Associated with Trauma

Research is now underway to determine which factors involved in stalking are most likely to cause physical and emotional trauma in victims. In the SVP, several factors were found to be positively related to physical trauma. Jealous individuals were likely to inflict physical trauma on their victims in cases of domestic violence and stalking (Morewitz, 2001d). SVP Case 121C shows how an incident of jealousy resulted in physical trauma. In this case, Ms. E, had been in a dating relationship with Mr. F. Late one night, she returned to her residence and found the offender waiting for her. He accused her of having sex with another man and that since she was giving it away, he would get some too. In spite of her denial and request to leave her alone, the offender threw her down and raped her.

Relationships that involve arguments over finances, family responsibilities, and other issues are positively associated with physical trauma. In SVP Case 249C, a simple argument over going to the store resulted in physical trauma. Mrs. G did not want to go to the store with her husband, Mr. H, because she had chores to do at home. The suspect said that he was the man of the house and then threw his wife down and raped her.

Offenders in the SVP with a history of violence were more likely than those without such a history to commit violence that resulted in physical trauma to the victims of stalking and relationship violence (Morewitz, 2001d).

Conclusion

The physical and emotional effects of stalking on the victims and their families and friends are traumatic and should not be underestimated. The effects parallel those who are the victims of PTSD and other severe injuries and disorders. Research is needed to identify which characteristics worsen the physical and emotional effects of stalking. Additional research on the types of stalking, the nature of the offender/victim relationships, and the characteristics of the stalkers and survivors will provide new data on the association between stalking and trauma.

5

Non-Legal Responses to Stalking

This chapter focuses on the types of non-legal strategies used by stalking victims. Little is known about how victims use non-legal approaches to stop stalking. The type of offender/victim relationship, duration and severity of the stalking, and characteristics of the offenders and victims may affect which approaches, if any, are employed. Stalking survivors may be alarmed and confused about the stalker's bizarre and erratic behaviors. The threats and stress of stalking may be so debilitating that they are unable to respond adequately to the stalking. The extreme and chronic nature of stalking may lead to anxiety, depression, Post Traumatic Stress Disorder, and other stress-related health problems, which prevent the stalking victims from adequately responding to the stalker. Stalking victims who suffer from these types of disorders may be more likely to allow the stalking to go on unabated or delay in taking any action to combat the stalking. In some circumstances, the offenders may see the victim's lack of a response as a signal that they are interested in pursuing a relationship.

Despite the psychological stress of stalking, many survivors select some type of coping strategy. Cupach and Spitzberg (1998) suggest that stalking victims typically use five strategies: (1) directly interact with the offender, (2) seek legal protection, (3) avoid the stalker, (4) retaliate against the perpetrator, and (5) rely on technology for protection. In other instances, the stalking targets may be at a lost as to what to do to stop the stalking.

Stalking targets also may obtain informal support from family, friends, and co-workers and counseling from mental health professionals and clergy. In addition, the victims cope with the trauma of stalking by contacting physicians and other health care professionals. Another response which has been largely ignored in research is that the victim may reconcile with the offender (Fremouw, et al., 1997, p. 668).

Direct Interaction

Victims frequently will interact directly with stalkers to curtail their behaviors. They will tell them not to continue their stalking and harassment. They may send a letter or e-mail the offender as well. In a survey of stalking on one college campus, Fremouw, et al. (1997) noted that one of the top five coping strategies of both male and female victims was confronting the offender (Fremouw, et al., 1997, p. 668).

In 6% of the cases in the Stalking and Violence Project (SVP), the victims told the offenders to go away or leave them alone (See Appendix B). Frequently, the stalking, harassment, and physical abuse persist despite the victim's rejections and may increase as a result of this direct repudiation. For example, SVP Case 101C shows that the stalking and harassment increased after the victim told him to go away. Ms. A, a graduate student, initially gently refused Mr. B, another graduate student whom she had dated four to five times and who lived in Ms. A's building. She continued to gently reject Mr. A's overtures but he continued to stalk her. Finally, she met with him and explicitly told him that she did not wish to be involved with him in any way. However, instead of complying with her wishes, Mr. B stalked and harassed her for a period of four years.

In addition, stalking targets will ask third parties to warn the offender. In Fremouw, et al. (1997)'s investigation, having someone warn the stalker was selected as a strategy by both female and male victims (Fremouw, et al., 1997, p. 668).

Avoidance and Indirect Approaches

Cupach and Spitzberg (1998) noted that the victims of intrusion often use indirect and avoidance strategies. Jason, et al. (1984) found that 32% of females who were harassed for more than one month by a former date did not respond to the harasser. Eight percent of the victims in this study reported being mean and distant with their former dates. Werner and Haggard (1992) reported that in a study of persons who were coping with unwelcome intrusions on the job that the victims preferred indirect types of avoidance and rejection.

Cupach and Spitzberg (1998) suggest that the victims of unrequited love also rely on passive and indirect approaches to deal with their pursuers. They may avoid telling the offender that they are not interested in seeing the person or that their behaviors are intrusive. Moreover, the victims may find ways to avoid having interactions with the stalker. These passive and indirect approaches are used to avoid hurting the feelings of the pursuer. Yet, because these indirect approaches give mixed signals to the pursuer, the rejector's message actually facilitates and intensifies the individual's obsessional behaviors (Cupach & Spitzberg, 1998, p. 254).

In Fremouw, et al. (1997)'s survey of stalking on a college campus, both male and female victims frequently changed their schedule to avoid the stalker (Fremouw, et al., 1997, p. 668). Both female and male victims also will simply ignore phone calls from stalkers (Fremouw, et al., 1997, p. 668). Stalking victims go to great lengths to escape their perpetrators (NIJ, 1998; Pathe & Mullen 1997; Hall, 1998). In the NVAW survey, 11% of the victims changed their address, 11% moved out of town, and 7% avoided the offender (NIJ, 1998, p. 19). Thirty-seven percent of the victims in Pathe and Mullen (1997)'s study changed their jobs, school, or career in response to the stalking (Pathe & Mullen, 1997, p. 14).

In the SVP, 10% of the victims reported that they left their residence to escape the perpetrator. In SVP Case 230C, Ms. Y, who was pregnant with the offender, Mr. Z's child, fled their shared residence with her two children after he stalked and assaulted her. A few months previously, the victim had been hiding from the perpetrator by sleeping with her 5-year-old son, and he came in and began choking her. She almost passed out and developed bruises under her jaw and collarbone.

In the NVAW study, 4% moved into a shelter, and 5% altered their driving habits to avoid the stalker (NIJ, 1998, p. 19). Thirty-nine percent of the victims in the Pathe & Mullen (1997)'s investigation relocated between one and five times, 7% moved between states, and 3% went overseas (Pathe & Mullen, 1997, p. 14). In Fremouw, et al. (1997)'s survey, male victims occasionally changed their phone numbers and addresses to avoid the offenders (Fremouw, 1997, p. 668). It is interesting to note that female victims in the study did not choose these strategies in dealing with their stalkers.

About 7% of the targets in the SVP study obtained temporary shelter. Temporary shelter included staying at the house of a friend or relative home or domestic violence shelter. In SVP Case 180C, Ms. C had to stay at a friend's house to escape being stalked, assaulted, and raped by a boyfriend of Ms. D, her female relative. Ms. C complained that Ms. D had tried to control her life, threatened to kill her, and verbally abused her. She stated that Ms. D had her boyfriend stalk, assault, and attempt to rape her. Because of the stress of this persistent stalking and attacks, the victim has lost various jobs.

Targets will change their identity, e.g., change their names to avoid the offender. They even will change their physical appearance to keep their stalkers from finding them. Hall (1998) described how several victims altered their appearance by dyeing their hair, putting on weight, and reducing their breast size so that their perpetrators would not recognize them (Hall, 1998, p. 134).

Retaliation

The targets of stalking may retaliate against their perpetrators. They may physically assault, shame, or ridicule the offender to curtail their unwelcome and intimidating behaviors. Fremouw, et al. (1997) reported that male victims occasionally had someone else assault the offender (Fremouw, et al., 1997, p. 668). In Pathe and Mullen (1997)'s research, 65% of the victims had considered using violence to retaliate against the stalker. Mullen and Pathe (1997) reported that one woman considered going out with a knife as the offender stood loitering outside (Pathe & Mullen, 1997, p. 14). The victim may vandalize the offender's property as well. They also may get back at their perpetrators in other ways. Victims who share children with their perpetrators may seek child custody to protect their children and possibly retaliate against the offenders who also want custody of their children. Additional research is needed to find out how victims retaliate against perpetrators.

Safety and Security Strategies

Victims frequently take advantage of available security devices and technology to protect against stalkers. Available technology includes telephone caller ID and call back features and Internet security features that protect against stalking. In the NVAW study, 22% of the victims reported taking extra precautions (NIJ, 1998, p. 19). Seventy-eight percent of the stalking targets in Pathe and Mullen (1997)'s study increased their security. They used unlisted phone numbers, post office boxes, security systems for their residence, guard dogs, and other security precautions.

Ten percent of the targets in the SVP stated that they employed various strategies, including changing the locks at home, monitoring phone messages, and carrying protective sprays. In SVP Case # 205, Ms. E used pepper spray to fend off Mr. F, her former spouse, who one day ran after her and grabbed her. Ms. E complained that Mr. F has stalked and attacked her in the past. In response to his on-going stalking and attacks, she has called 911 and filed a second order of protection against him.

The NVAW researchers found that 17% of the victims obtained a gun (NIJ, 1998, p. 19). Forty-five percent of the victims compared to 29% of the non-victims carried something to defend themselves (NIJ, 1998, p. 19). Fremouw, et al. (1997) found that carrying a repellent spray was one of the top five responses of female victims. Carrying a whistle or other type of alarm was a less frequently used strategy by female victims than by male victims (Fremouw, et al., 1997). Pathe and Mullen (1997) noted that 5% of the victims took self-defense classes and 6% obtained weapons. Fremouw, et al. (1997) reported that arranging for a personal escort at times was one of the top five responses of female victims (Fremouw, et al., 1997, p. 668). Victims also may hire a private investigator (Pathe & Mullen, 1997, p. 14). In the NVAW study, less than 1% hired a private investigator, and less than 1% had their public records sealed (NIJ, 1998, p. 19).

Seeking Guidance and Counseling

Victims frequently must cope with bizarre and erratic behaviors on the part of the stalkers and may not know how to best deal with the offenders. The targets may seek counsel and guidance from friends and co-workers. In Pathe and Mullen (1997)'s study, 78% of the victims sought assistance from family and/or friends (Pathe & Mullen, 1997, p. 14). Nineteen percent obtained advice from co-workers or supervisors (Pathe & Mullen 1997, p. 14). They found that stalking victims infrequently sought the assistance of colleagues and supervisors at work. Victims also seek advice from their clergy (Pathe & Mullen, 1997, p. 14).

In addition, stalking victims also may contact professional counselors and therapists to help them ascertain the offender's motivations and effective ways to terminate the stalking. Counselors and therapists utilize acute and long-term psychosocial therapies to help stalking victims cope with the psychological terror of stalking and gain clarity on how to respond to the stalker.

About 3% of the victims in the SVP reported that they sought counseling. In SVP Case 96, Ms. G obtained counseling to cope with the extreme stress of her stalking victimization. Ms. G was afraid to go out of her house because she feared that Mr. H, who had children in common, was stalking her and her children and posed a danger. One day, the offender came to her home, demanding that she come outside to talk to him. Previously, she had been physically assaulted by the offender.

Medical Care for Stalking Victims and Offenders

Victims who are injured by their stalkers will seek medical care for their injuries. Little is known about what percentage of injured stalking victims obtain medical care for their injuries. In the SVP, approximately 10% of the stalking targets reported receiving medical care for injuries caused by the perpetrators. There is also little known about the conditions under which injured victims obtain medical care for their injuries. In addition, there are no studies that deal with the injuries sustained by the stalkers.

Moreover, it is not known what proportion of stalking targets seek advice about their stalking victimization from medical professionals. Pathe and Mullen (1997) found that 44% of the stalking victims in their study consulted with medical practitioners, a majority of whom were primary care physicians (Pathe & Mullen, 1997, p. 14). It is not clear what proportion of these persons also had been assaulted by the offenders.

Reconcialiation with the Stalker

Fremouw, et al. (1997) found that among male and female college students, male victims frequently reconciled with the perpetrator, whereas female victims were less likely to do so (Fremouw, et al., 1997, p. 668). Other studies of stalking have not reported reconciliation as a frequent response of stalking victims. Fremouw, et al. (1997)'s findings may be unique to male college students who are victims of stalking as a result of having been in primarily heterosexual dating relationships.

Factors Related to the Victim's Use of Non-Legal Strategies

To date, there has been little research on which psychosocial and financial factors are associated with the victim's selection of non-legal strategies to curtail stalking. As noted earlier, anxiety, depression, PTSD, and other disorders may impair the victims' use of adequate coping strategies. The type of relationship and the attributes of the offenders and victims also may affect which non-legal strategies are selected. According to the SVP results, the type of relationship is associated with certain victim responses. Married persons were more likely to leave home in response to the stalking than those victims who had been in dating relationships. Married persons have few if any ways to escape the stalker. Even if the stalker is separated from the victim, the offender may still have a house key or access to family members who can let them into the victim's residence. The offender is likely to know the victim's routines and whereabouts and changing residence may be the only way to escape from the stalker. In contrast, those in dating relationships tend not to be as accessible as married persons since they live in different residences from the stalkers.

Persons in dating relationships were more likely to employ monitoring and safety strategies than married persons. The victims of date stalking may rely on security procedures since they will not know of the stalker's whereabouts and the likelihood of future stalking. Thus, the safety procedures will help keep the victim isolated from the offenders and prevent them from knowing the victim's location. In contrast, married persons may be less likely to use security and safety precautions since they will be less effective in curtailing their spouses' stalking and harassment. The victims may view security and safety precautions as ineffective since their spouses already will have greater access to their homes and know their regular activities.

Other aspects of the victim-offender relationship also may affect whether safety precautions are taken. For example, the ways in which stalking targets respond to the perpetrator may be associated with the victims' use of safety strategies. SVP victims who responded to the stalkers by telling them to go away were more likely to use safety precautions.

As noted previously, Fremouw, et al. (1997) reported some gender differences in victim responses to stalking on a college campus (Fremouw, et al., 1997, p. 668). Male victims most frequently selected the following non-legal strategies: (1) confronting the offender, (2) ignoring the perpetrator, (3) making up with the stalker, and (4) altering his schedule to avoid the offender. Female stalking victims were most likely to choose the following strategies: (1) ignoring the offender, (2) confronting the perpetrator, (3) changing her schedule to avoid the offender, and (4) carrying pepper spray or other spray weapon (Fremouw, et al., 1997, p. 668).

The SVP results showed that both female and male victims of multiple stalking were likely to use safety and security strategies to cope with multiple forms of stalking. However, it was not possible to determine if there were gender differences in which types of safety and security methods were used by the stalking victims.

A variety of financial, social, and psychological factors may account for why certain stalking victims use domestic violence shelters while others do not. Stalking victims represent a subset of victims of domestic violence. Stalking survivors and other domestic violence victims who rely on domestic shelters tend to come from low socio-economic status groups (Sullivan & Rumptz, 1994). These persons frequently do not have the financial resources to move their residence easily and are less able to hire attorneys to combat their assailants than those with more financial resources.

The socioeconomic status of stalking victims also may be related to their use of other safety and security strategies. According to SVP findings, victims of multiple stalking who lived in census tracts with low median incomes were more likely to use self-protection procedures. These findings suggest that the use of safety and security procedures are not necessarily limited by limited financial resources. There are, in fact, many security strategies that do not require significant expenditures. With regard to middle and upper income groups in the SVP, there were an insufficient number of victims in the upper-income census tracts to determine if upper-income victims also relied on self-protection strategies to combat multiple stalking.

Data are now being collected on the characteristics of stalking victims who seek psychological counseling and support. In the NVAW investigation, 30% of the female victims and 20% of the male victims reported obtaining psychological counseling because of the stalking (NIJ, 1998, p. 19). Roberts and Dziegielewski (1996) noted that several factors are likely to bring stalking victims into counseling. They found that the three most common conditions are: (1) escalation of the frequency or severity of the stalking, (2) injuries inflicted on the victim by the stalker, whether they are intentional or accidental, and (3) disruptions in relationship and work.

In addition to focusing on victim characteristics and attitudes, the demographic and social attributes of the offenders may be associated with whether victims rely on safety and security strategies. The ethnic background of the stalkers may be related to whether the stalking victim used non-legal strategies in coping with the stalker. In the SVP, the ethnic background of the offenders was related to the victim's use of security procedures. When African-American offenders stalked their victims in variety of ways, the stalking targets were likely to use safety and security procedures. In contrast, there was no association between multiple stalking by White and Hispanic offenders and the victim's use of safety procedures.

Moreover, the offenders' social and psychological problems may be related to whether the victims rely on safety precautions. For example, in the SVP, stalking victims were more likely to rely on security strategies if the stalkers were suffering from mental illness. In addition, the relationship between using safety procedures and having a jealous stalker approached statistical significance.

Conclusion

Are direct responses to stalkers more effective than indirect methods? Is guidance from friends and co-workers as effective as counseling from professionals? Unfortunately, research to date has shown that neither approaches are effective (Cupach & Spitzberg, 1998, p. 255). Jason, et al. (1984), in a study of women who were harassed after ending a relationship with men, reported that direct approaches were no more effective in stopping the intrusions than passive styles of responding. Likewise, studies of sexual harassment also show that confronting the perpetrators directly was no more effective than indirect techniques (Livingston, 1982).

6

Stalking Law and Victims' Use of the Courts

History of Stalking Laws

Since the late 1980s, stalking has been the subject of movies, television, radio broadcasts, Internet web sites, magazines, newspapers, and books. The deadly consequences of many stalking cases plus the helplessness of many stalking victims are now topics of public debate. Thus, the media has brought to consciousness a social issue that had been hidden in previous years. The public awareness of stalking and similar harassment behaviors was first brought to the forefront in the 1980s (Lowney & Best, 1995, pp. 33–57; Morewitz, 1996).

While the media focus on stalking began in the late 1980s, stalking had been a problem for celebrities and others for years. In the past, these persons had suffered in relative silence because there was no societal recognition of the problem and consequently little effective law enforcement. In the 1990s, in response to publicized stalking cases, stalking laws began to be enacted. The 1989 murder of actress Rebecca Schaeffer by Robert John Bardo, a 19-year-old unemployed fast food worker and obsessed fan, catalyzed the California legislature to pass the first anti-stalking law (Miller, 1993, p. 1303).

In 1993, the U.S. Congress held hearings with stalking victims and then passed legislation that directed the National Institute of

Justice to develop a model anti-stalking code (Hearing Before the Committee on the Judiciary United States Senate, 103rd Congress, 1st Session on Combating Stalking and Family Violence, Anti-stalking Proposals. March 17, 1993; NIJ, 1993; NIJ, 1996). The Model Anti-Stalking Code was designed to help states enact consti-tutional and enforceable anti-stalking laws (NIJ, 1993, p. 5). The Attorney General, acting through the Director of the National Institute of Justice, was mandated to: (1) evaluate existing and pro-posed laws, (2) formulate a Model Anti-Stalking Code, (3) dissemi-nate findings to state officials, and 4) report to Congress on the Project's findings. All states now have anti-stalking statutes.

The Model Anti-Stalking Code made a number of recommen-dations for improving law enforcement efforts in order to mini-mize risks to stalking victims and enhance the enforcement of state laws. The Code recommended a multidisciplinary approach, utiliz-ing the police, counselors, social service organizations, and victims assistance groups (NIJ, 1993, pp. 50–51, 70). It also offered guide-lines on classifying stalking offenses, using enhanced penalties, notifying victims of the release of convicted stalkers, providing mental health evaluation and treatment of offenders, and restrict-ing the conditions under which convicted stalkers are released. In addition, the Code called for training police officers, using protec-tive orders, creating department policies and procedures for han-dling stalking, and establishing systems to record and keep track of stalking offenses.

In 1994, the Violence Against Women Act (VAWA), Title IV of the Violent Crime Control and Law Enforcement Act of 1994, was passed to facilitate law enforcement efforts in the area of violence against women, including stalking and domestic violence (NIJ, 1998, preface) and expand the availability and scope of relief pro-vided to the victims of violence. The Act seeks to increase collabo-ration among the police, prosecutors, victims advocates, and members of the judiciary. The U.S. Department of Justice, Office of Justice Programs offers resources to initiate programs and fund research. In response to Subtitle F of the VAWA, an annual report to Congress must be made to share research on effective strategies for dealing with stalking. In addition to violence against women, Congress in 1998 directed the Attorney General to evaluate existing or proposed legislation dealing with child victims of stalking.

Public concern over stalking has reached other countries. In November 2000, Japan passed a new anti-stalking law, and its national police established a task force to combat stalking (New York Times on the Web, Breaking News From A.P., Nov. 24, 2000, pp. 1–3). As in the case of the U.S., the murder of a woman by a stalker catalyzed public outcry in Japan, leading to the enactment of Japan's anti-stalking law. Forty officials from the National Police Agency were assigned to investigate stalking complaints and develop a national database of stalkers.

With the increased access to the Internet, electronic stalking has developed as a social problem. There are now 26 statutes in the United States that specifically prohibit electronic stalking (National Conference of State Legislatures, www. ncsl.org). California, New York, and Massachusetts are three of the states that include online stalking in their statutes. Electronic stalking may involve harassment but not necessarily explicit threats. In other states, existing anti-stalking laws may be used to prosecute Internet stalking.

Before Anti-Stalking Legislation Was Enacted

Before the enactment of anti-stalking statutes, most threatening behaviors were not punishable unless the victims were physically harmed (Strikis, 1993, p. 2774). In California, a stalker's threat would be classified as a violation only if the victim was aware that the threat would be carried out immediately (Cal. Penal Code 422 (Deering Supp. 1993)). In the past, what sanctions did exist, usually were light. For instance, in Alabama, harassment, e.g., striking, pushing, or kicking a person is a Class C misdemeanor (Ala. Code 13A-11-8 (a), 1992). In addition, law enforcement officials had been reluctant to enforce the existing laws. This was especially true in cases involving persons who had been in relationships. Prosecutors were hesitant to charge offenders in domestic relationships even when the victim had been assaulted (Strikis, 1993, p. 2774; E. Topliffe, 1992, pp. 1041–1042). Judges were reluctant to hand down harsh sentences in wife battering cases (Fain, 1981, pp. 497, 562).

In previous years, stalking victims could avail themselves of protective orders and other civil remedies (NIJ, 1990). However, obtaining these orders was a burden to victims involving time lost and extra legal expenses. Moreover, the police and courts were reluctant to enforce the protective orders.

The police and judiciary did not understand the psychology inherent in domestic violence and stalking syndromes and consequently were wary of placing restrictions on a person's behavior. Strikis (1993) described the case of a judge who denied a protective order and instead ordered mediation for a man who kidnapped and sexually assaulted his ex-girlfriend (Chicago Tribune, Sep. 27, 1992 at C4; Chicago Tribune, Sep. 30, 1992 at C5).

Benefits of Anti-Stalking Laws

Anti-stalking laws have the following advantages. First, they make the public aware of the serious implications of stalking. That should lead to stronger enforcement of protective orders.

Second, they offer more greater protection of victims' rights by handing down harsher penalties for repeat offenders than traditional protective orders and harassment laws did (Strikis, 1993, p. 2778).

Third, they protect victims by enabling the police and courts to intervene before a stalker's threats can escalate to physical violence (Strikis, 1993, p. 2779).

Fourth, some anti-stalking laws are helpful because they provide for mental health treatment and psychological assessment for the stalkers.

Fifth, the laws may require court supervision of the perpetrators and the threat of criminal sanctions, which were lacking under previous protective orders and harassment laws (Strikis, 1993, p. 2779). For stalking victims who do not seek retribution, these additional levels of protection may be sufficient. For example, in Florida, a stalking target did not want her estranged husband go to prison for a long time. Instead, she sought court supervision and isolation from the perpetrator (St. Petersburg Times, Dec. 8, 1992 at Citrus Times 1; Strikis, 1993, p. 2779).

Sixth, they can be an effective deterrent for some would-be stalkers (Strikis, 1993, pp. 2780–2781). Strikis (1993) notes that for certain criminals, the threat of loss of respect associated with being jailed or imprisoned and the resulting public condemnation is sufficient for them to stop their stalking (Strikis, 1993, p. 2781).

Finally, they provide for arrest and imprisonment of incorrigible offenders.

Criticisms of Anti-Stalking Statutes

Various criticisms have been leveled against anti-stalking laws. First, they have been criticized for duplicating statutes already on the books that deal with stalking and related behaviors.

Second, anti-stalking laws have not demonstrated their effectiveness in curtailing stalking (Strikis, 1993, p. 2779), and critics assert that ineffective law should be repealed.

Third, anti-stalking statutes criminalize behaviors that frequently involve persons in intimate relationships, and this results in unwarranted governmental intrusion into private lives.

Finally, some opponents believe anti-stalking laws to be unconstitutional. The laws have been characterized as vague and overly broad. Other opponents assert that the laws provide for unconstitutional detention of suspects.

Legal Elements of Stalking in State Statues

California enacted the first anti-stalking law and, because it is comprehensive and well-written, it has served as a model for other states (Boychuk, 1994, pp. 774–775). California's law consists of three basic requirements: (1) the act, (2) the threat, and (3) the intent.

The act. The suspect must willfully, maliciously, and repeatedly follow or harass another person.

The threat. The perpetrator must make a credible threat against the victim.

Intent. The suspect must have an intent to cause the victim to reasonably fear death or bodily injury.

According to Boychuk (1994), stalking statutes in other states can be classified into three groups based on California's three requirements. Like California, Alabama, Arkansas, Iowa, Colorado and other states require all three elements. Other states, including South Dakota, Delaware, and Illinois, require either an act or a threat in addition to intent. Connecticut, Idaho, and Louisiana are some of the states that require both an act and intent.

The Act of Stalking

Some states include specific behaviors such as "harassing" in their statutes, while other states use broad descriptions such as "engaging in conduct." Most U.S. states use the term, "following," as part of their stalking statute or similar terms such as "lying in wait," "placing under surveillance," and "pursuing." Two states, Minnesota and Kentucky, do not define the behavior; they merely make it illegal to stalk another individual. Many states, including California, Florida, Michigan, and Rhode Island, include the term, "harassing," in their laws. West Virginia and Kansas require that the suspect both follow and harass the victim.

Many states forbid broader behaviors than the California law and may face constitutional threats. For example, many states forbid conduct or a course of conduct. Several statutes forbid actions that are similar to behaviors classified under tort notion of assault. Other behaviors, such as appearing for no legal purpose in proximity to the victim's residence or work setting, are prohibited in various statutes.

The Threat of Stalking

A number of states differ from California's credible threat requirement. Some states such as Delaware require the element of threat as an alternative to other behaviors. The Delaware statute requires following and harassing behaviors or repeated credible threats with criminal intent. Other states, such as Connecticut, Georgia, and Kansas, do not have a threat requirement. The Connecticut law requires intent and willful and repeated following that causes the victims to reasonably fear for their safety.

The Intent of Stalking

The intent requirement in stalking laws can be classified into two types: those that require merely general intent and those that also require specific intent. States such as Idaho, Illinois, and Iowa have general intent requirements. For example, Idaho requires that the perpetrator willfully, maliciously, and repeatedly follow or harass the victim.

States such as Connecticut and Texas have specific intent requirements in their statutes. These states require that the suspect intends to have some specific effect on his victim, such as to annoy, alarm, or cause emotional distress.

In most states, the suspect must have committed behaviors or acts that, when considered as a whole, constitute a pattern of behavior. Some states, including Colorado, Illinois, Michigan, and North Carolina, require that the offender engage in two acts at different times. States classify stalking as a variety of acts, ranging from specific acts, e.g., lying in wait, to general forms of behavior, e.g., harassment.

State Penalties for Stalking

Stalking statutes have been classified based on sentencing systems, which vary by state (Tucker, 1993, pp. 617–618). Some states make all acts of stalking a misdemeanor, others categorize initial acts as a misdemeanor and subsequent violations as a felony, while others classify all violations as a felony. In many states, convictions can result in a misdemeanor or felony. A person convicted for a misdemeanor can receive a jail sentence of up to one year in many cases, while a felony conviction often carries a sentence from 3 to 5 years (NIJ, 1996, p. 7). In a majority of states, the convicted stalkers can receive a sentence enhancement if they had engaged in certain offenses, such as displaying a weapon or violating an order of protection. A prior stalking offense can result in increased sentences. In 14 states, the prior stalking offense must involve the same target. In some states, the convicted stalker faces an enhanced sentence of up to 10 years in prison for repeat offenses.

Convicted stalkers can receive mandatory minimum sentences. The Massachusetts's state law has a mandatory minimum sentence for convicted stalkers (Mass. Gen. Law Ann. Ch. 265 43 West Supp. 1993; Miller, 1993, p. 1315). In addition, an individual convicted of stalking faces a 1-year mandatory minimum sentence for violating a protective order or an injunction. A repeat offender receives a 2-year mandatory minimum sentence.

States have other criteria for determining sentencing. Connecticut has harsher penalties for those convicted of stalking minors (Conn. Gen. Stat. Ann. 53a-181c, West Supp. 1993; Miller, 1993, p. 1315). Stalking a child under the age of 16 is classified as a felony and is punishable by up to five years in prison. In contrast, stalking an adult is a misdemeanor and is punishable by up to one year in prison.

Parole or Probation and Mental Health Referrals

Various state anti-stalking statues provide for mental health treatment and/or psychological assessment as a condition of parole or probation (Ill. Ann. Stat. Ch. 720, paras. 5/12-7.3, 5/12-7.4; Miller, 1993, p. 1310). In Illinois, the sentencing court authorizes the parole board to require a convicted stalker to participate in psychological treatment as a prerequisite for parole or probation. Likewise, Hawaii authorizes the sentencing court to require mental health treatment for convicted stalkers (Haw. Rev. Stat. 711–1106.5 Supp. 1992).

Constitutionality of State Stalking Laws

In the 1990s, legislatures were faced with the complex task of enacting anti-stalking statues that could defeat constitutional challenges (NIJ, 1996, pp. 6–7). It is sometimes problematic to differentiate lawful conduct and stalking behaviors. In 1993, when the Model State Anti-Stalking Code was published, no appellate court decisions had been handed down. Three years later, 53 constitutional challenges had been initiated in 19 states. However, the courts generally have supported the laws. Constitutional attacks have centered around two issues: the laws are overly broad and/or vague. Other constitutional issues deal with notice to the suspect, ascertaining probable cause in stalking arrests, restrictions on bail, and exclusion of certain types of behaviors and categories of victims.

Overly Broad Laws

A law will be found unconstitutional by being overly broad if it prohibits conduct that is protected by the First Amendment.

These protected behaviors include the exercise of free speech and the right to lawful assembly. The courts have applied this doctrine only as a last resort. A law that appears overly broad can survive a constitutional challenge if a limited interpretation of the law has or could have been applied. In addition, overly broad statutes will survive constitutional challenges unless they pose a major threat to protected behaviors under the First Amendment.

Some anti-stalking statutes have safeguards to protect constitutionally protected behaviors such as labor picketing or other lawful demonstrations (Strikis, 1993, pp. 2786–2788). Other anti-stalking laws protect conduct associated with the conduct of lawful businesses such as private detective and news work. Those laws that do not have express exclusions might be perceived as unconstitutional. Strikis (1993) points out that Florida's law may criminalize the behaviors of a television crew which follows a public figure. A prosecutor probably would decide not to bring charges in this case. The possibility that a law will be misapplied does not make the statute invalid on the basis of overbreath.

Some critics suggest that even statutes with express protection should be held unconstitutional because they are overly broad. Anti-stalking laws may be similar to Loper v. New York City Police Dept., which found that broad restrictions on begging violates the First Amendment. In this case, the court favored the rights of beggars in balancing the interests of the beggar, the beggar's audience, and that of the government. Strikis (1993) suggests that anti-stalking laws would not face the same legal outcome. A person who goes out in public is considered to have a "diminished privacy interest" and, therefore, is expected to permit certain invasions of privacy in public settings. In addition, a potential listener of a beggar in a public space is not considered a captive audience. A person has the freedom to simply walk away from the street beggar. In contrast, a stalking victim, under the Florida statute, becomes a captive audience if he or she is willfully, maliciously, and repeatedly followed and does not have the ability to curtail the behaviors. Therefore, stalking under the Florida law and similar statutes may not violate the First Amendment violations of free expression.

People v. White is an example of a case where the stalking law was not struck down because of the overly broad challenge (People v. White, 536 N.W.2d 876 (Mich.App.Ct. 1995); NIJ, 1996, p. 7).

In this Michigan case, the suspect was convicted of attempted aggravated assault. The defendant had called his ex-girlfriend as many as 100 times per week at home and on the job, threatening her and her family. He tried to get the law overthrown, arguing that his First Amendment right to free speech was denied since the victim could not determine which of his telephone calls were acceptable and which were illegal. The court upheld the law since the suspect's repeated calls to the target (sometimes 50 to 60 calls a day) and his threats to kill her and her family were not protected speech. The court noted that it is the aim of the law to prevent such behaviors because the threats of violence in these types of cases can lead to the victim's death.

In another stalking case in Michigan, the Sixth U.S. Circuit Court of Appeals upheld the constitutionality of the state's anti-stalking law, which prohibits people from making unwanted contact with a victim two or more times and making at least one credible threat (New York Times on the Web, Breaking News from A.P., 2001, pp. 1–3). In 1994, Jerry Lee Staley was accused of breaking into his ex-girlfriend's home, telephoning her as many as 15 times a day, chasing her with a baseball bat, and threatening to cut her stomach with a knife. In 2000, the U.S. District Court ruled in the defendant's favor, asserting that the law was written so broadly that it could be used to convict those persons in legitimate occupations, such as journalists and private investigators, who follow individuals as part of their job. However, the Sixth U.S. Circuit Court of Appeals ruled that Mr. Staley's behavior fell within the purview of the state's anti-stalking statute. In addition, the appellate court held that the anti-stalking law protects legitimate behavior even though it does not define the phrase, "conduct that serves a legitimate purpose."

Anti-stalking laws also may seem to restrict a person's constitutional right to freedom of movement (Strikis, 1993, p. 2788–2789). A person has the inherent right to walk down any public street. However, if a person is following someone repeatedly, then he or she may be arrested under certain anti-stalking statutes. Under some laws, another required element is a reasonable fear that the following was an intentional threat.

Although freedom of movement is not mentioned in the Constitution specifically, it has been considered a basic constitutional right. Yet, this long-held right can be limited if there are compelling public safety concerns. Under certain laws, persons who follow other individuals in a willful, malicious, and repeated manner and place them in fear do not have a right to stalk.

Anti-stalking laws could restrict a person's First Amendment right of freedom of association. The U.S. Supreme Court has held that certain intimate relationships must be protected against the State's undue interventions. A person who stalks may be in an intimate relationship with the victim, and, therefore, may have a certain right of freedom of association. Strikis (1993) notes that the government is not interested in regulating intimate relationships per se. Instead it seeks to control dangerous behavior on a wide scale. Therefore, stalking in intimate relationships, if it involves threats that place a person in fear, will not be protected under the First Amendment.

Vague Laws

The courts rarely have nullified anti-stalking laws on the basis of the vagueness challenge. A criminal law must have sufficient definiteness so that the public can know what behaviors are illegal and be protected from arbitrary and discriminatory law enforcement (Strikis, 1993, pp. 2790–2795). In addition to specifying what behaviors are illegal, the statute must offer guidelines to facilitate fair law enforcement. Criminal laws that are vague violate the Fourteenth Amendment, Due Process Clause.

For instance, in People v. Holt, the suspect claimed that the Illinois anti-stalking statute was unconstitutionally vague (People v. Holt, 649 N.E. 2d 571 (Ill.App.Ct. 1995; NIJ, 1996, p. 7). He was convicted of being in violation of a restraining orders by repeatedly visiting a skating rink where his ex-girlfriend had been taking private lessons and staring at her during her lessons. The court upheld the law, concluding that the statute adequately warns innocent individuals which activities are prohibited: making threats, following, or keeping someone under surveillance, and it is reasonably expected that these behaviors will cause fear and intimidation. The court noted that the law does not depend solely on subjective criteria. Instead, it establishes objective standards for evaluating the offenders' conduct and impact of their behaviors on the victims.

Boychuk (1994) suggests that having a threat requirement helps laws withstand constitutional attacks on the basis of being vague and overly broad. A stalker who threatens another person generally is aware that such communications constitute a crime. Strikis (1993) argues that the burden of proof should not be on the police to determine if the suspect's activities are threatening for this allows the police to exercise too much discretion, which can lead to arbitrary enforcement of the law. Rather, the statutes should require that the suspect make a direct or indirect threat (Strikis, 1993, p. 2795). Despite the advantage of having a threat requirement, Louisiana, Nebraska, and other states have removed it from their statutes.

Another challenge facing anti-stalking statutes is that they can be judged to be unconstitutionally vague if the definitions contained in the laws lead to subjective interpretations (Strikis, 1993, p. 2792). Statutes that define "harassment" according to definitions used in federal laws, which define harassment as a course of conduct that causes the victim to experience substantial emotional distress, would survive constitutional challenges. However, those laws that do not offer guidance about what behaviors conform to the standard of behavior may not survive.

The term, "following," provides more opportunity for subjective interpretation, especially in statutes that only require the term, "following," in their definition of stalking. For example, a husband who is separated from his wife and children might be considered to be stalking if he simply drives by his former residence to check on his children. Strikis (1993) indicates that in considering terms such as "following," the courts reviews them in light of the law's legislative history and previous judicial rulings.

Intent

Boychuk (1994) points out that stalking laws that have specific intent requirement can overcome constitutional scrutiny on the basis of vagueness. An offender who has a specific intent to cause a particular effect presumably is on notice that his or her behaviors are illegal. Criminal liability should be based on the suspect acting purposefully, knowingly, and negligently (Strikis, 1993, pp. 2793–2794).

The standard of repeated and malicious behavior is meant to be consistent with the standards set by the Model Stalking Code (NIJ, 1993; NIJ, 1996).

The presumption of intent has been established in state statutes to make it easier for the prosecution to prove the suspect's intent (Miller, 1993, pp. 1326–1328). However, according to Miller (1993), these statutory presumptions may violate the Due Process Clause of the Fourteenth Amendment if they shift the burden of proof to the defendant. The statutory presumptions in the stalking laws of Michigan and Washington may not survive constitutional scrutiny.

Providing Notice to the Suspect

Strikis (1993) notes that suspects have a constitutional right to be provided fair notice for their violations, and the adequacy of this notice is evaluated based on the charges made (Strikis, 1993, pp. 2796–2797; United States v. Nat'l Dairy Prods. Corp., 372 U.S. 29, 32–33 (1963)). The Fifth Amendment to the Constitution provides that persons may not be denied due process, and under this requirement, persons are entitled to fair notice of which conduct is prohibited (NIJ, 1993, p. 10). Providing notice to suspects is affected by the evolving public and court perceptions of stalking (Strikis, 1993, pp. 2796–2797). As the public develops an awareness of which types of behaviors constitute stalking, offenders will be less able to argue that they are unaware that their behaviors are illegal. Public perceptions of stalking thus protect against legal attacks claiming that the anti-stalking laws are vague.

Probable Cause in Stalking Arrests

Legislators in certain states know that stalking can lead to serious injuries or death, and have passed laws to allow the arresting officer to arrest a stalking suspect without a warrant (Wis. Stat. 29.05 (1m) (1992); Fla. Stat. Ann. 784.048 (5) West (1992); Strikis, 1993, pp. 2797–2798). The U.S. Supreme Court prefers that the police use arrest warrants when feasible. However, certain anti-stalking laws allow the police to arrest the suspect without a warrant when the facts and conditions lead the officer to believe that the suspect has committed an offense.

The issue of "probable cause" raises concern about the arbitrary arrests of persons in violation of their constitutional right to due process. The "probable cause" difficulty can come into play under certain conditions, e.g., when false allegations are made by individuals who have been in prior relationships. An officer's determination of "probable cause" will be judged in light of whether the arrest was considered objectively reasonable (Malley v. Briggs, 475 U.S. 335, 341 (1986); Strikis, 1993, p. 2798).

Restrictions or Denial of Bail and Use of Illegally Obtained Evidence

Some state legislators recognized that stalking suspects can continue to pose an immediate threat to their victims even after they have been arrested. Therefore, stalking laws have been enacted to restrict or deny bail to suspects or otherwise limit the pretrial release of suspects (Strikis, 1993, pp. 2798–2801). In North Carolina, a stalking case actually ended in the victim's murder. A man was arrested for threatening his ex-wife. After being arrested, he reportedly told the police that he would get even with his estranged wife. Seven days later, he killed her in front of their 4-year-old daughter and also wounded his ex-wife's friend (State v. Holder, 418 S.E. 2d 197, 201 (N.C. 1992)).

In Illinois, bail can be denied to a stalking defendant based on a hearing (Ill. Ann. Stat. Ch. 725, para. 5/110-4 Smith-Hurd 1993). The procedures for this hearing are similar to those of a criminal trial except the prosecution may use illegally obtained evidence to deny bail to the suspect (Miller, 1993, p. 1311). If the court denies bail, it must bring the detained suspect to trial within 90 days of the detention order.

A victim in Ohio can ask for an anti-stalking order of protection as a condition of a pre-trial release for the defendant, in addition to any other restrictions imposed by the bail (Miller, 1993, p. 1311). The court may hand down such an order if it believes that the defendant poses a threat to the victim. The order may prohibit the suspect from visiting the alleged victim's home, workplace, or school (Ohio Rev. Code Ann. 2903.211-.215-Baldwin Supp. 1992; Miller, 1993, p. 1311).

The Illinois statute has been considered excessive by critics. However, other states are looking into the effectiveness of restricting bail through anti-stalking laws or other statutes (Strikis, 1993, p. 2798; Miller, 1993, p. 1310). These state laws could be modeled after the Federal Bail Statute that allows judges to limit access to bail if no condition of release would guarantee the safety of the victim and others (18 U.S.C. 3142 (e) (1988); Strikis, 1993, p. 2799). The Federal Bail Statute offers safeguards that include the right of the suspect to testify and cross-examine witnesses.

Strikis (1993) notes that the constitutionality of pre-trial detention could be raised if the states assert the right to detain stalking suspects but not other dangerous defendants. Also, if a state such as Illinois allows for the use of illegally obtained evidence in pre-trial detention hearings for stalking defendants but not other dangerous defendants, then the laws may be unconstitutional (Ill. Stat. Ch 725 para. 5/110-4 Smith-Hurd, 1993).

Exclusion of Categories of Behaviors and Persons

Some state anti-stalking laws may face constitutional attacks because they do not specify certain offender behaviors, such as threats to rape and sexually assault a victim (Strikis, 1993, p. 2803). Oklahoma's statute limits application of criminal penalties to violations of orders of practice (Okla. Stat. tit. 60.11 (Supp. 1993)). Other statutes may not withstand constitutional scrutiny because they restrict the type of victim or offender that can be included. The Oklahoma anti-stalking law limits offenders to adults, emancipated minors and 16-year-olds. The West Virginia law restricts victims of stalking to those who have been engaged to be married or in a previous relationship with the perpetrator (West Virginia Code 61-2-9a (a) 1992; Strikis, 1993, p. 2804).

Other Possible Constitutional Challenges

Anti-stalking laws may bring on other constitutional challenges. For example, the sentences handed down to convicted stalkers may be attacked for violating the Eighth Amendment to the U.S. Constitution, which prohibits cruel and unusual punishments (NIJ, 1993, p. 11). Double jeopardy is another problem associated with anti-stalking statutes. According to this principle, a person cannot be convicted twice for the same crime. However, certain anti-stalking laws allow for criminal contempt charges for violations of protective orders as well as charges for criminal stalking offenses. These types of issues raise constitutional questions that may result in court challenges.

Federal Stalking Law

In 1993, Congressman Ed Royce and Senator Barbara Boxer proposed legislation to make stalking a federal crime (H.R. 740, 103d Cong., 1st Sess. (1993); Miller, 1993). Their efforts were part of a strategy to deal with the ineffectiveness of protective orders in handling stalking. Critics at the time pointed to the ineffectiveness of new state and federal laws in deterring emotionally troubled offenders.

Stalking victims in the U.S. actually have several federal statutes to protect them against certain forms of stalking (U.S. Department of Justice, 1999 Report on Cyberstalking, pp. 15–18). Under 18 U.S.C. 875 (c), it is federal crime, punishable by up to five years in prison and a fine of up to $250,000 for using interstate or foreign commerce to communicate a threat of physical harm to a person. This law can apply to both electronic and non-electronic stalking. However, it only prohibits communication which involve actual threats; it does not refer to a pattern of conduct that is meant to harass or annoy an individual. It does not prohibit Internet stalking that involves posting harassing and menacing messages on electronic bulletin boards or in chat rooms.

Other forms of stalking are prohibited under 47 U.S.C. 223, which makes it a federal crime, punishable by up to two years in prison, to use a telephone or telecommunications device to harass or threaten any person. The law also requires that the offenders had attempted to remain anonymous.

In 1996, President Bill Clinton signed the Interstate Stalking Act, which prohibits an individual from traveling across state lines to injure or harass another person and place that person or their family members in reasonable fear of death or bodily injury (18 U.S.C. 2261A). A number of serious stalking cases have been prosecuted under this statute.

Two year later, President Clinton signed into law 18 U.S.C. 2425, which makes it illegal under federal law to use interstate or foreign commerce to knowingly solicit or entice a child into sexual activity. This law prohibits the use of the Internet or other forms of communication by pedophiles. However, the statute does not protect children from harassing communications unless there is evidence that the perpetrators intended to entice or solicit the minor for sexual activities.

Attorney General Janet Reno, in her 1999 report on Internet stalking, concluded that there were still gaps in federal anti-stalking law. Although many cases of stalking, including Internet stalking, come under the purview of local and state jurisdictions, the U.S. Attorney General concluded that many instances of stalking involving third parties fall outside federal jurisdictions. For example, federal laws do not currently outlaw the posting of harassing and menacing electronic communications on Internet bulletin boards and in electronic chat rooms that use third parties to stalk and harass other persons. Attorney General Reno also called for enhanced penalties when the victim is a minor because of the greater vulnerability of children. The Attorney General asserted that these legislative changes can fill existing gaps without displacing local and state law enforcement efforts while still maintaining First Amendment safeguards.

With regard to First Amendment protections, the U.S. Supreme Court has recognized that the First Amendment does not limit any and all laws that may have an impact on speech. In terms of its implications for stalking, the high court in Watt v. United States, 394 U.S. 705 (1969) (per curiam) held that the government may prohibit true threats without violating the First Amendment. Thus, stalking, which can consist of true threats of violence, can be criminalized without adversely affecting an offender's First Amendment rights.

The federal government has identified the Internet as a significant instrument for protecting speech (Reno v. American Civil Liberties Union, 521 U.S. 844, 850–52, 870 (1997); American Civil Liberties Union v. Reno, 31 F.Supp. 2d 473, 476, 493 (E.D. Pa. 1999).

Federal anti-stalking laws need to balance the need to have First Amendment protected speech on the Internet and in other forms of interstate and foreign commerce with the need to protect stalking victims. Therefore, Attorney General Reno called for states to update their anti-stalking statutes to include electronic communications and also ensure that they were not so broad that they had a chilling effect on free speech.

Stalking Victims' Use of the Courts

With the enactment of anti-stalking laws, there has been a significant increase in the number of stalking targets who seek police assistance and court protection. According to the National Institute of Justice (1998) telephone survey of 8,000 women and 8,000 men, the police referred about 24% of stalking complaints to a prosecutor or court (NIJ, 1998, p. 16). Females (24%) who reported stalking complaints to the police were somewhat more likely to be referred to a prosecutor or court than male stalking targets (19%). The police may take stalking complaints from women more seriously than from men. This is also evidenced by the fact that female stalking targets (25%) were more likely to report that their perpetrator was arrested than male stalking victims (17%).

For many years, victims of domestic violence have been able to file orders of protection in an attempt to keep their perpetrators from committing further abuse. Pennsylvania passed the first law in 1976 to provide for orders of protection in cases of domestic abuse against spouses and other partners (National Council of Juvenile and Family Court Judges, 1992; Klein, 1996, p. 192). These protective orders are the primary way of protecting domestic violence victims in many states. In Massachusetts, 45,515 protective orders were issued against offenders in 1992 (Klein, 1996, p. 192).

Since the passage of anti-stalking laws, domestic courts in various states are now asking victims who file protective orders to report if they have been stalked. These data provide a rich account of the conditions leading up to the victim's filing orders of protection and the social and demographic characteristics of the alleged stalking victims and perpetrators.

The results from the recent Stalking and Violence Project (SVP) showed that 65% of the victims who filed orders of protection in domestic court requested court protection against stalking. This is compared to 29% of the sample who reported being stalking victims. Ninety-one percent of the victims who requested stalking protection also requested protection against physical violence.

The factors related to seeking court protection are unknown. A number of conditions may influence whether stalking targets seek court protection against their offenders. The type of relationship between the victim and the stalker, the type, severity, and duration of the stalking and/or domestic violence, and victims' perceptions of the effectiveness of the court are conditions that can determine whether court protection is sought. Moreover, the social characteristics of the victims and offenders may influence the extent to which court protection against stalkers is requested.

The SVP found that the type of relationship, the forms of stalking behaviors, kinds of violence, and other conditions were related to whether court protection was requested. In regard to type of relationships, individuals in dating relationships were more likely than married persons to seek court protection against stalking. These findings suggest that persons in dating relationships may feel more threatened by their perpetrators or feel that they have less to lose by filing protective orders than married individuals. Married persons may be less likely to perceive their partners' behaviors as constituting stalking than persons in dating relationships. Moreover, those individuals who had terminated their relationship with the offender were more likely to file for court protection against stalking than those who had not. Victims may fear that ending the relationship had increased the danger to themselves and their family and therefore view court protection as essential.

In the SVP, the type of stalking and related offenses were positively related to seeking protective orders. The actions of stalkers who intruded into the victims' home and workplace and harassed the target at home by telephone were positively related to requesting court protection. Victims who had their property vandalized by the offender were more likely to seek court protection against stalking than those who did not have their property vandalized.

It is interesting to note that two other offender behaviors were associated with the victims' decreased use of the court for stalking protection. Stalking victims were less likely to seek court protection against stalking for perpetrators who used alcohol and drugs. These findings suggest that the perpetrators' chronic use of alcohol and drugs may be related to decreased motor activity, leading to a reduction in stalking behaviors. In addition, once the offenders were arrested, the victims decreased their use of court protection.

Effectiveness of Stalking Laws and Orders of Protection

To what extent do stalking laws and orders of protection actually protect stalking victims? Insufficient research is available to answer this question. However, data are available in the related field of domestic violence, where a number of studies have shown that perpetrators frequently violate protective orders by not only approaching their victims, but even continuing to assault them (Harrell & Smith, 1996; Klein, 1996).

In an investigation of 355 women who filed temporary restraining orders, Harrell and Smith (1996) discovered that 77% of the women reported that perpetrators had violated the protective orders during the first three months after the temporary order had been filed (Harrell & Smith, 1996, p. 221). During the first year of the temporary protective orders, 80% of the women stated that their offenders had violated the order by contacting them. Seventy-five percent of the women also reported that permanent orders of protection were violated through illegal contacts by the offenders. Some of these contacts consisted of attempts at reconciliation. Fifteen percent of the women indicated that the offenders had moved back into their residence during the first three months of the protective order, and 13% stated that they had reconciled with the perpetrators.

Harrell and Smith (1996) found that four types of abuse occurred after a temporary restraining order had been handed down: (1) severe violence, (2) other forms of violence, (3) threats of violence and property damage, and (4) psychological harassment (Harrell and Smith, 1996, p. 223). During the year after a restraining order was issued, 9% of the women reported severe physical violence. The most prevalent offender behavior was psychological abuse (57%). As part of this psychological abuse, more than 15% of the women stated that the perpetrator stalked them.

Similarly, Klein (1996) showed that offenders continue to abuse their victims after restraining orders were filed. In a study of restraining orders issued in Quincy Court in Massachusetts in 1990, the researcher reported that almost 50% of the perpetrators committed additional abuse against their victims during a two-year period following the restraining order (Klein, 1996, p. 1999). In fact, about 49% of the offenders were arrested for assaulting their victims and about 40% for violating the Abuse Prevention Act-209A. In addition, victims took out new restraining orders against 95 offenders for committing new offenses. An additional 146 per-petrators were arrested for new crimes that were unrelated to the victim. Re-abuse tended to occur during the first 90 days following the issuance of a restraining order.

Keilitz, et al. (1998), in a study of three jurisdictions, discov-ered that persons who had obtained temporary or permanent restraining orders reported that their sense of well-being had increased as a consequence of obtaining the protective order. Seventy-two percent of the individuals one month after obtaining a protective order and 65% in the 6-month follow-up assessment stated that they no longer had any difficulties with their abusers (Keilitz, et al. 1998, p. 3). Seventy-two percent of victims at the initial interview stated that their quality of life had improved. Six months later, 85% of the victims reported improvement in their quality of life, more than 90% stated that their self-esteem was higher, and 80% reported feeling safer.

However, certain forms of abuse increased from the time of the initial interview to the 6-month follow-up. Stalking increased from 4% to 7%, psychological abuse went up from 4% to 13%, unwel-come telephone calls went up from 16% to 17%, and physical abuse increased from 3% to 8%.

Conclusion

Stalking parallels sexual harassment which previously remained outside of public consciousness. Increasingly, the media, because of its ability to reach millions of people quickly, has educated the public about the dangers of stalking. With the globalization of communica-tion and the increased accessibility of the Internet, stalking awareness now goes well beyond the confines of the United States. In this way, the media and technological innovations in communication have accelerated the pace and dynamics of social change in inter-personal relationships.

Widespread enactment of anti-stalking laws and the involvement of the criminal justice system are playing an important role in promoting social change in face-to-face interactions. The U.S. Congress enacted federal anti-stalking laws that supplement local and state laws.

The women's, victims rights, and anti-violence movements also have impacted social change for these movements form the ideological basis for the development of anti-stalking laws and community-based responses to stalking.

7

Police Intervention

In the past and even until the early 1990s, the police were reluctant to make arrests for domestic violence because of societal norms that regarded family violence as a private, family matter (Hutchison, et al., 1994, p. 301). The police have been frustrated because few domestic cases were prosecuted successfully (Abrams & Robinson, 1998, p. 478). Instead of arresting the assailants, the police had been trained to calm down the individuals involved in domestic disputes and refer them to social services (NIJ, 1986, p. 3; Hutchison, et al., 1994, p. 301). With increased public awareness of the harmful effects of domestic violence, the police non-arrest strategy has been criticized for treating domestic violence less seriously than violence involving strangers and failing to protect domestic violence victims (Hutchison, 1994, et al., p. 301).

Before the enactment of anti-stalking laws, stalking targets, like victims of domestic abuse, had to endure their problems without the aid of much effective police intervention. Stalking by ex-lovers or dates was regarded as a normal infatuation that eventually resolved itself (Abrams & Robinson, 1998, p. 478). A lovesick person or rejected lover was more to be pitied than sanctioned. Stalking survivors had to use laws dealing with harassment, trespassing, invasion of privacy, intentional infliction of emotional distress, obscene and harassing phone calls, and related criminal and civil laws (Dietz, 1984, p. 516). This points to the need for early and aggressive police intervention to minimize further victimization

(Williams, et al., 1996). The Federal Bureau of Investigation (FBI) found that 30% of all women murdered in 1990 were killed by their husbands and boyfriends, and as many as 90% of these victims were stalked before their murder (Hearing Before the Committee on the Judiciary, U.S. Senate, March 17, 1993, p. 10).

In 1993, the U.S. Congress held hearings to consider the scope of the problem facing stalking victims. The Committee on the Judiciary, U.S. Senate, heard the testimony of individuals including Helen M. Lardner, whose sister, Kristin, was killed on a busy Boston street in 1992 (Hearing Before the Committee on the Judiciary, U.S. Senate, March 17, 1993, p. 33). Ms. Lardner testified that her sister would still be alive today if the court had either checked the record of her sister's stalker, Michael Cartier, or notified the police when she sought a temporary restraining order against the offender. Kathleen Krueger, the wife of a senator, also testified that she and her family were stalked for over eight years by Thomas Michael Humphrey, a pilot who flew a plane for her husband's political campaign (Hearing Before the Committee on the Judiciary, U.S. Senate, March 17, 1993, p. 27). The Krueger family was told repeatedly that law enforcement could not intervene until the suspect attempted to inflict physical harm.

Today, under some anti-stalking laws, a pattern of behavior and evidence of intent to cause harm are sufficient grounds for an arrest (NIJ, 1996, p. 9). The police no longer need to wait for the perpetrator to "do something" before making an arrest. They now can arrest the offender, stopping the behavior temporarily.

Since the passage of anti-stalking laws, there has been an increase in the number of stalking incidents reported to the police (NIJ, 1998, p. 16). The National Violence Against Women (NVAW) survey found that stalking incidents occurring after 1995 were more likely to be reported to the police than those taking place before 1990. The NVAW survey attribute this increase to the enactment of anti-stalking legislation. California was the first state to pass such laws in 1990, and by 1995, all states and the District of Columbia had passed anti-stalking laws.

With the increase in police reporting, there is a need to understand police policies and procedures and the factors which affect police intervention and its effectiveness (NIJ, 1993). In 1993, the U.S. Congress directed the National Institute of Justice (NIJ) to develop a model anti-stalking code and training program to assist states in enacting effective legislation. Under the direction of NIJ, the National Criminal Justice Association (NCJA), in collaboration with the Police Executive Research Forum, surveyed police chiefs in the U.S. and abroad in order to examine the range of police responses to stalking and ways to protect victims. Other surveys such as the 1998 NVAW study and Tucker (1993)'s survey of law enforcement agencies in Florida also have assessed the role of the police in responding to stalking incidents.

Police Policies and Procedures

According to the NIJ (1993) survey of police chiefs, most police agencies with or without stalking laws responded to stalking in similar ways (NIJ, 1993, p. 39). Forty-seven percent of the police chiefs surveyed indicated that investigators or detectives investigate stalking complaints, whereas 23% stated that patrol officers investigate the incidents. The respondents stated that police domestic violence units and crimes against persons units rarely participate in these investigations.

The NIJ (1993) survey of police chiefs found that those involved in investigating stalking complaints frequently had not received training on how to handle stalking incidents. For those agencies with anti-stalking laws, 53% do not offer formal anti-stalking training and 86% without such laws do not provide training. The stalking training that does occur is generally incorporated into the training of recruits, in-services, roll-call, and special instructional programs.

After a police report had been made, the survey found that 82 percent of the agencies in states with anti-stalking laws and 60% without such laws indicated that they do follow-up investigations. For those agencies which do follow-up investigations, 74% with anti-stalking laws and 93% without laws stated that they keep information on subsequent telephone calls to the victim.

According to the survey results, police agencies with or without anti-stalking laws utilize a variety of interventions in dealing with offenders (NIJ, 1993, p. 40). Those with anti-stalking laws use certain alternative charges against offenders more than those who do not have such laws. In states with anti-stalking laws, 81% of the agencies charged suspects with trespassing, whereas 74% of those agencies without such laws charged these persons with trespassing. Seventy-four percent of the police agencies with anti-stalking laws filed assault charges against the perpetrators, whereas 60% of those agencies without such laws filed assault charges against them.

Tucker (1993) found that more stalking charges initially were filed by the Florida state attorney's office than the number of offenders arrested for stalking (Tucker, 1993, p. 647). This occurred because the police provided the Florida state attorney's office with information on all possible charges, and that office determined which charges would be prosecuted. The police in a few instances arrested the perpetrators on charges other than stalking because they were uncertain about the Florida anti-stalking statute.

Although there has been an increase in the number of stalking incidents reported to the police since the enactment of anti-stalking laws, the actual number of stalking arrests has not increased (NIJ, 1998, p. 16). The NVAW study found that some police were more likely to arrest or detain a suspect if female victims were involved than if there were male victims involved (NIJ, 1998, pp. 15–16). The suspect was arrested or detained in 16.7% of the cases in which male victims were involved, compared to 25.1% of the cases in which female victims were associated with the case. Moreover, the police were more likely to refer women to victim services than men.

The police can use their discretion in handling stalking incidents because in many cases there are insufficient grounds for them to take action or they lacked effective policies and procedures (Tucker, 1993, p. 669). When the stalker flees the scene, it makes it difficult for the police to question him or her and assess the accuracy of the complainant.

In the NVAW survey, the most common police response (68% of the cases) was to take a report from the victim (NIJ, 1998, p. 16). Other frequent police responses consisted of giving advice on self-protective measures (33.2%) and referring the case to the prosecutor or court (23.3%). In 16.7% of the stalking incidents, the police did nothing. The least frequently used police response was referring the victim to victim services (13.8% of the cases).

Stalking Behaviors That Resulted in Police Intervention

According to the NIJ (1993) survey findings, stalkers were most likely to follow their victims, make threatening and abusive telephone calls, vandalize the victim's property, visit their work place, and assault them (NIJ, 1993, p. 41). Stalkers also gave unwelcome gifts, such as dead animals, falsely accused them of improper and illegal actions, and left threatening or annoying notes on their automobiles. In Florida, Tucker (1993) found that the most frequently occurring behaviors that involved police contacts were: persistent following, telephone harassment, verbal abuse, assault, and trespassing (Tucker, 1993, p. 645).

Hutchison, et al. (1994) noted that, contrary to the popular image of life threatening domestic violence, a majority of police contacts deal with less serious forms of domestic violence. However, findings from other studies did not support this hypothesis (Hutchison, et al., 1994; Burgess, et al., 1997; Morewitz, 2000a; Morewitz, 2000b). Burgess, et al. (1997) found that 30% of those charged with felony domestic violence reported that they had engaged in stalking behaviors. Offenders with a history of prior assaults also were likely to stalk their targets.

In the Stalking and Violence Project (SVP), stalking victims who were involved in police contacts were likely to be the targets of serious violence and sustained physical and emotional trauma (Morewitz, 2000a; Morewitz, 2000b; See Appendix B). Stalking survivors in these cases were subjected to extensive verbal abuse and threats and were likely to be hit, pushed, and had weapons used against them.

According to the SVP results, stalking targets who were both threatened with physical harm and then assaulted were likely to be involved in police contacts. In SVP Case 428SF, Mrs. P was threatened with physical harm, physically assaulted, stalked, and raped by her husband, Mr. Q. She finally contacted the police after being raped.

In the SVP, the precipitating events for police intervention, however, were not always acts of physical violence or threats of physical harm. Vandalism and thefts were positively associated with calling the police (See Appendix B-SVP Case 337C).

The SVP found that the police assistance was obtained more often when the perpetrator had committed other crimes. Offender crimes associated with police intervention included: having an out-standing warrant, cocaine abuse, rape, and kidnapping. In SVP Case 472SF, Ms. R was raped, physically abused, and kidnapped for two hours by Mr. S, who formerly had lived with the victim and had been engaged to her. Subsequently, the suspect was arrested and jailed for a period of time.

The SVP findings showed that being stalked and assaulted by a jealous partner or date frequently triggered police involvement. These individuals can be jealous and fearful of abandonment (See Appendix B).

Other factors increase the probability that stalking targets will seek police assistance. Burgess, et al. (1997) reported that among some offenders charged with felony domestic violence offenses, stalking was more likely to occur when "love turned to hate" (Burgess, et al., 1997, p. 396). The authors also revealed that perpetrators with known alcohol abuse problems were likely to stalk their victims, and victims with known alcohol and drug abuse difficulties also were at high risk of being stalked. However, alcohol and drug abuse by stalkers in the SVP did not increase the chances of police contacts.

The findings from the SVP showed that pregnant stalking victims were more likely to be involved in police contacts than non-pregnant stalking targets. Pregnant women feel more vulnerable for themselves and their future babies and, therefore, may be more likely to contact the police.

The Gender of Stalking Victims Involved in Police Contacts

According to the NVAW study, 55% of the female and 48% of the male victims indicated that their stalking problems were reported to the police (NIJ, 1998, p. 15). Out of those cases that involved police intervention, most of the stalking victims (84% female and 75% male) said that they personally contacted the police. In the remaining cases, other persons reported the stalking to the police. The NVAW findings for female stalking victims are identical to the percentage of females victimized by single violent offenders in the National Crime Victimization Survey (NIJ, 1998, p. 15). Tucker (1993) reported that the majority of stalking victims involved in police assistance and orders of protection were women (Tucker, 1993, pp. 645–646).

In Pathe and Mullen (1997)'s study, 69% of the stalking victims indicated that they had called the police. However, Fremouw, et al. (1997), in their survey of university students on one campus, found that seeking police assistance was one of the least used coping strategies for both female and male victims (Fremouw, et al., 1997, p. 668). Research is needed to determine if this pattern is unique to college populations or typical of this age group.

The SVP found that 31% of the stalking victims who had filed orders of protection reported that the police had been contacted (Morewitz, 2000b). Of this group, 86% of the victims were female and 14% were male. These results are comparable to the gender distribution of all stalking victims in the sample. These findings differ significantly from the NVAW study and may be due to the fact that the SVP studied victims who filed orders of protection exclusively, whereas the NVAW surveyed many victims who did not file orders of protection.

SVP Case 67C illustrates a case in which a male stalking victim called for police assistance. Mr. G had been stalked, harassed, physically abused, and vandalized by his wife Mrs. H., who had been living at a different residence. Mrs. H had been stalking her husband wherever he stayed and had made harassing and threatening telephone calls. She had kicked and bit the victim, thrown objects at him, dropped a telephone on him, and smashed objects. The husband had requested a police escort every time he went to her residence to collect his personal items.

Police Intervention

The type of relationship between the victim and offender may affect whether police assistance is sought. The NIJ (1993) survey of police agencies found that the police responded to stalking complaints from people in different relationships (NIJ, 1993, p. 40). The survey found that stalking victims also included co-workers, neighbors, strangers, celebrities, and political leaders.

Likewise, Tucker (1993), in his survey of police response to stalking in Florida, found that the police encounter suspects who are in a variety of relationships. Although the anti-stalking law in Florida was aimed at ex-husbands and boyfriends, the police have arrested persons in other types of relationships, e.g., co-worker/supervisor, professional, and celebrity/fan (Tucker, 1993, pp. 645–646).

In terms of relationship status, Burgess, et al. (1997) found that stalkers involved in police contacts tended to live alone, not be married, and not live with children (Burgess, et al., 1997).

Of all the SVP stalking cases in which police assistance was sought, 24% of the victims were married and 40% were in current or past dating relationships. These data are comparable to relationship status of all stalking victims in the SVP sample. These results are similar to Hutchison, et al. (1994)'s study which found that police intervention frequently involve non-married (cohabiting) individuals.

SVP Case 121C is an example of a dating victim who called the police and filed a police report. Ms. A stated that one night at a night club, Mr. B, whom she had dated, approached her, yanked her hair, and said: "I'm not done with you." Ms. A's friends intervened, and Mr. B returned to his table. When she and her friends were leaving, Mr. B caught up with her, grabbed her by the arm and pinched her so hard that her arm was bruised. Ms. A ran out the door, chased by Mr. B, who could not catch her. Ms. A reported this incident to the police and charged him with simple battery (See Appendix B—Case Study 249C, which involved a spouse victim who was contacted by the police).

The SVP results indicate that the socioeconomic status of the victims may influence the process of obtaining police or other legal assistance. Stalking targets who were involved in police contacts were less likely to live in census tracts with low median incomes than all stalking victims in the study. Forty-one percent of the stalking victims involved in police intervention lived in census tracts with a median income of more than $39,999, whereas for all stalking victims in the sample, 10% lived in census tracts with a median income of more than $39,999.

The Social Characteristics of Stalkers
Involved in Police Contacts

A few investigations have assessed the social characteristics of stalkers involved in police contacts. Tucker (1993) reported that most stalkers appear to be normal and to come from a variety of socioeconomic status groups. While the majority of stalkers involved in police intervention are males, the police have arrested women who stalked men or women as well as men who stalked other men. Similarly, the SVP found that most of the stalkers associated with police contacts were males who had stalked females.

Tucker (1993) noted that stalkers have ranged in age from twelve to seventy-four. A 12-year-old boy in Escambia County, Florida, was charged with writing threatening notes to a classmate. A seventy-four-year-old man reportedly was charged twice with stalking a 10-year-old girl for over three months.

The SVP results revealed that since younger persons were more likely than older individuals to be involved in stalking and serious violence, they were more likely to be contacted by the police. Serious violence included using a weapon, hitting the victim, and threatening them with physical harm. In contrast, among older perpetrators, stalking was not related to these types of violence, and, therefore, the police were less likely to be contacted. An opposite trend, however, was revealed for one violent behavior, throwing objects at the victim. This was positively related to calling the police in the 41–60 offender age group, but not for the younger offender age groups.

In terms of the race of offenders involved in police contacts, Tucker (1993) reported that a majority of stalkers have been White (Tucker, 1993, p. 645). The SVP also investigated the ethnic/racial background of the offenders involved when police assistance was sought. The SVP findings provide partial support for the notion that there is a relationship between the ethnic/racial background of the offender and whether police assistance was sought. Forty-two percent of the African-American stalkers in the sample were involved in police contacts, while 51% of the total sample of stalkers were African-American. These results indicate that victims who were stalked by African-American offenders were somewhat less likely to be involved in police contacts. In contrast, targets who were stalked by White perpetrators were slightly more likely to be involved in police contacts. Thirty percent of the White stalkers were involved in police intervention, whereas 25% of the total sample of stalkers were White. There were negligible differences between the percentage of Hispanic stalkers involved in police calls (21%) and the total percentage of Hispanic stalkers in the sample (19%).

Reasons For Not Reporting Stalking to the Police

The reasons why stalking targets do not call the police may be similar to why domestic violence targets do not seek police assistance. According to various studies, domestic violence victims often do not call the police because they are inhibited by shame, embarrassment, and love for the perpetrator (Fleury, et al., 1998). In a survey of battered women in a shelter, Fleury, et al. (1998) found that respondents offered different reasons. They claimed that they were prevented from using the telephone and threatened with further violence. Only 3% of the women surveyed indicated that shame, embarrassment, or love were the only reasons for not calling the police.

Investigations of police contacts in stalking incidents reveal that, like domestic violence victims, stalking targets often do not seek police assistance (NIJ, 1998, p. 16; Tucker, 1993, pp. 646–647; Fremouw, et al., 1997). In the NVAW investigation, stalking targets who did not report their stalking victimization were asked why they did not report the stalking to the police (NIJ, 1998, p. 16). The results were as follows: (1) the victim did not consider the stalking to be a police matter (20%), (2) the police could not help (17%), (3) the victims were afraid of reprisals from the stalker (16%), (4) the targets took care of the problem themselves (12%), (5) the victims reported the stalking to someone else (7%), (6) the police would not believe the victims (7%), and (7) the targets thought that the problem was too minor (4%).

Tucker (1993) also noted that stalking targets often have been hesitant to file charges under the anti-stalking laws (Tucker, 1993, pp. 646–647). The victims may be fearful that it would prove to be too difficult to get the perpetrator arrested. Furthermore, stalking targets often are too afraid to confront the offender in open court. Stalking survivors may not understand the legal terms found in anti-stalking laws. This problem is compounded by the fact that police departments may not provide information on police policies and procedures to shelters, hot-lines, and other organizations which assist stalking victims. This may occur because not all police departments have shelters or other agencies in their jurisdictions, and the police departments themselves do not have adequate anti-stalking policies and procedures.

The victims' perceptions of racial and cultural discrimination may influence their decision to press charges against the stalker (NIJ, 1986, p. 3). People of color may be reluctant to file charges against their partners because they believe that people of color will receive harsher sentences (NIJ, 1986, p. 3). Those that do press charges may face the loss of social support from their family and friends within the minority communities.

The social environment may influence whether stalking targets contact the police. In a survey of stalking on a university campus, Fremouw, et al. (1997) found that female and male stalking victims felt that calling the police was not an effective strategy for stopping the stalking (Fremouw, et al., 1997, p. 668). These college students were more likely to confront the perpetrators directly, ignore them, and/or change their social environment to avoid offenders. Stalking incidents on college campuses seem to be in a unique category and these problems may be dealt with differently than in the general community.

Role of the Police in Stopping Stalking

The following factors affect whether arresting stalkers will protect stalking victims: (1) the nature of the relationship between the perpetrator and the targets, (2) the mental status and motivations of the offenders, (3) bail laws, and (4) the quality of the prosecutor's case (NIJ, 1996, p. 9). After an arrest, the prosecutor may be able to convince the offender to stay away from the victim. In some cases, the lack of effective responses from the police and courts have encouraged perpetrators to continue or even escalate their attacks (NIJ, 1996, p. 9).

In Sherman and Berk (1984)'s evaluation study of police responses to domestic violence in Minneapolis, the police had three options: (1) arrest the offender, (2) mediate and counsel both parties, and (3) keep the perpetrator away from the victim's home for several hours. The authors reported that arresting the assailant reduced subsequent offenses. However, research in other cities could not replicate these findings.

With the enactment of new anti-stalking laws, police agencies have had difficulty forming policies and procedures to deal with this newly defined crime. Police officers sometimes have to enforce potentially unconstitutional anti-stalking laws (Boychuk, 1994, p. 769). Furthermore, the definitions of stalking vary from state to state, and the understanding of the police regarding stalking laws varies considerably (NIJ, 1993, p. 75). It is not surprising that uniform investigation, arrest, and follow-up policies and procedures have not been established (Tucker, 1993, p. 656).

The police generally receive little training in how to respond to stalking complaints (NIJ, 1993, pp. 73–74; Tucker, 1993, p. 656). The police are trained to investigate a typical crime scene, collect evidence, and interview suspects and witnesses. However, they generally are not trained to collect evidence germane to stalking, assess the potential threat of a stalker, or know that the stalking law has been violated and make appropriate arrests. The training that the police do receive occurs during roll-calls, in-services, and at the police academy (NIJ, 1993, p. 75).

Wright, et al. (1995) suggest that stalking crimes are a separate category with different crime scene indicators, investigative consideration, and search warrant considerations depending on the nature of the stalking, e.g., domestic vs. non-domestic stalking (Wright, et al., 1995, pp. 38–43). In non-domestic stalking, stalking is ongoing and does not have a traditional crime scene. Stalking will occur at the victim's home, workplace, or other setting. At some point in time, the offenders may communicate with the target and may later remind the target of this event to further terrorize the victim. Investigators should consider tracing telephone calls and conducting a threat analysis of written and telephone communications. The investigator should interview the victim about possible accidental contacts with the stalker. In obtaining a search warrant, the police should consider a wide array of materials, including diaries, newspapers, logs, telephone records, and returned letters.

In cases of domestic stalking, the investigators are more likely to find a traditional crime scene. The crime scene may be the victim's home and/or work place. Domestic stalking can be associated with violence, and the crime scenes will reflect the disorder of domestic violence. There may be weapons present, and the crime scenes may reveal an escalation of violence and its resulting trauma. Other family members and friends may be the victims of violence as well. If the victims have used safety and security precautions, the stalkers may have access to them only at their work settings. As a result, co-workers, and security workers also may become victimized by the perpetrators. The stalkers may not be at the scene when the police and emergency medical teams arrive. Investigators should consider domestic stalking if there is a history of domestic violence involving the victim and the suspect, and this is evidenced by past and present restraining orders and police reports. A common element of this form of stalking is a history of conflict due to various stressors, including financial problems, jealousy, and substance abuse. In addition to evidence found at the immediate crime scene, investigators should research court, medical, and financial records to corroborate premeditation on the part of the suspects.

Additional specialized police units should be established to assess threats and follow up on stalking cases (Tucker, 1993, p. 686). For example, the Los Angeles Police Department formed the Threat Management Unit in 1990 to better deal with the problems posed by stalkers (NIJ, 1996, p. 5). Since 1986, the U.S. Secret Service has run an interdisciplinary consultation program that assists Secret Service agents in identifying individuals who may pose a threat to the President or other officials (NIJ, 1993 p. 73).

Moreover, personnel with specialties in the behavioral sciences and forensics are needed to assist the police in investigating stalking complaints. The police need to know about the available resources in the community, such as domestic violence shelters, hot-lines, and self-protective measures for the victims.

Orders of protection are an important arsenal for the police. Orders of protection notify the perpetrators that their behaviors are unwelcome, and that if they continue, they will be subject to arrest (NIJ, 1996, p. 9). However, the police and courts frequently are unable to enforce orders of protection even though in most states they can make warrantless arrests if there is probable cause that the suspect violated the order (NIJ, 1993, p. 77). Furthermore, the large number of orders of protection in effect at any given time makes it difficult for the police to enforce them (Strikis, 1993, p. 2774).

For example, the Illinois State Police stated that there were 35,346 reported violations of orders of protection over a period of only five months (Strikis, 1993, p. 2774; Fountain & Kirby, 1992, p. D1).

Violating an order of protection in many states is a misdemeanor. However, criminal felony charges can be filed instead of a misdemeanor charge. One of the consequences of only having civil sanctions is that information about any past violations of the orders of protection may not be recorded since they are not criminal offenses (Thomas, 1993, p. 127). Therefore, the police often will not know the stalking history of potentially dangerous suspects (NIJ, 1993, p. 83).

The Massachusetts state police established the first computer database to follow up offenders who have orders of protection taken against them (Tucker, 1993, p. 651). A system for tracking orders of protection across states would be helpful in monitoring stalkers and collecting evidence against them.

Stalking victims can increase the chances that the police will arrest their stalkers if they themselves collect evidence against the suspects (NIJ, 1996, p. 11). The New Mexico Department of Public Safety Training Center, in collaboration with the State's Coalition Against Domestic Violence, developed a "Stalking Critical Incident Diary." This diary allows the stalking target to document the time, location, and type of stalking.

Community policing is another promising method of dealing with stalking and domestic violence (NIJ, 1996, p. 10). The concept of community policing encourages the police to resolve problems in the community on a proactive basis instead of simply responding to calls for police assistance. According to this strategy, the police work with community groups and leaders to identify and resolve local problems and assess the effectiveness of their efforts.

Some police departments are using experimental, community-based techniques to better respond to stalking and domestic violence. Police agencies are preparing location histories that document all law enforcement responses to a given residence. The police also are helping stalking survivors obtain restraining orders and find safe houses.

Victims' Perceptions of the Effectiveness of the Police

A key source of data on the effectiveness of police responses comes from surveys and interviews of stalking victims. These data provide first-hand views of the effectiveness of the police and clarify the results from other studies. NVAW investigators surveyed the attitudes of stalking victims who reported that the police were contacted. Fifty percent of these victims were satisfied with the police actions (NIJ, 1998, pp. 16–17). Fifty-four percent of the respondents stated that their situation had improved after the police had been contacted and 51% thought that the police did everything that they could to deal with the problem. Respondents who reported that their stalkers were arrested were much more likely to be satisfied (76%) than those who reported that the offenders were not arrested (42%).

For those who believed that the police should have done more, the NVAW researchers asked the stalking victims to give specific examples. A majority of these respondents (42%) felt that the offender should have been arrested and 20% stated that their complaint should have been taken more seriously (NIJ, 1998, p. 17). Other suggestions included: offering protection to the victim (16%), giving the suspect a warning (14%), and being more supportive toward the respondent (13%). Only 5% of the respondents indicated that the police should have forced the perpetrator to go away.

The Attitudes of Police Chiefs Regarding Police Effectiveness

Another source of data on police effectiveness comes from the police agencies themselves. Police chiefs and the officers who respond to stalking incidents provide useful evaluation data about the strengths and weaknesses of law enforcement. The 1993 NIJ survey of police chiefs found 86% of the officials in states with anti-stalking laws believed that the intervention alternatives available to them were adequate. They indicated that charging suspects with multiple offenses improved the probability that the perpetrator would be stopped (NIJ, 1993, p. 40). In contrast, only 43% of the police chiefs in states without anti-stalking laws believed that their intervention options were satisfactory.

Thirteen percent of those police chiefs with anti-stalking laws who believed that intervention alternatives were satisfactory recommended that specific behaviors needed to be defined as stalking to minimize confusion with other offenses. Some police officials indicated that their anti-stalking laws were too vague, broad, or difficult to prosecute. Other respondents stated that it would be useful if the laws did not require witnesses or police presence at the time of the crimes. Certain police chiefs noted that potential targets such as children and acquaintances are not included in anti-stalking laws.

Some police chiefs with anti-stalking laws recommended new tactics. One recommendation was that the courts require stalkers to submit to psychological evaluations. A second suggestion was that uniformed patrol officers should follow up after the complaint has been filed. Police chiefs also recommended that the courts should require stalkers to wear electronic monitoring devices. Furthermore, the respondents suggested that certain forms of harassment be included in the anti-stalking laws (NIJ, 1993, p. 41). These forms include: watching and waiting repeatedly, behaviors that are harassing even though no credible threats have been made, and repeatedly appearing at the victim's work place.

Tucker (1993), in his survey of law enforcement agencies in Florida, found that the police needed better training and more comprehensive policies (Tucker, 1993, p. 649). There is significant variability in the understanding of anti-stalking laws among agencies and officers. A survey of police officers' awareness of domestic violence legislation in Texas also showed the necessity for police training (Tucker, 1993, p. 649; Eigenberg & Moriarty, 1991, pp. 102–109). More than one third of the police officers did not know that they could make a warrantless arrest for domestic violence that takes place outside their view (Eigenberg & Moriarty, 1991, pp. 102–109).

Tucker (1993), like the NIJ (1993) survey, found that the police departments have difficulty monitoring stalkers after their release from police custody (Tucker, 1993, pp. 649–650). Police departments reported having trouble gaining access to orders of protection to determine if they had been violated by the suspects.

In Florida, police agencies and victim advocate organizations have supported the Florida anti-stalking law despite the difficulties in enforcing the statue (Tucker, 1993, pp. 654–655). They reported that the statute may be fair if it is moderately used in cases where the stalker has carried out a pattern of harassment merely for the purpose of threatening the victim. The respondents believed that although the law may be less useful in dealing with chronic stalkers, it may be useful in responding to former lovers.

Conclusion

The establishment of anti-stalking legislation has led to new efforts on the part of law enforcement agencies to respond to stalking incidents. With these new laws, come the problem of understanding and enforcing them. Additional training, follow-up, monitoring, and community-wide policing should improve the way the police and community respond to stalking and offer victims new protection against their perpetrators. As specialized police units and interdisciplinary teams of specialists disseminate their research findings to police agencies nation wide, local law enforcement agencies will be better able to respond to stalkers.

The availability of the new laws and more constructive police responses should increase the number of stalking targets who will seek police assistance. Such factors as the type of violence, the stalking victims' racial/ethnic and socio-economic status characteristics, perceived threats associated with stalking, and the type of offender/victim relationship should be considered when developing effective police responses. The process whereby stalking victims, their family members, neighbors, and others obtain police assistance need to be explored further to determine better ways to prevent stalking-related injuries and fatalities. Future research should focus on the impact of policing on the motivation of stalkers.

8

Treatment and Incarceration

Access to Counseling for Stalking Victims

Counseling and therapy for stalking victims should be comprehensive, a combination of advice on practical safety and security procedures, victim education, and supportive psychotherapy (Abrams & Robinson, 1998, pp. 478–479). However, stalking targets frequently do not seek counseling or are unable to obtain access to such services. In the past, the lack of public awareness about stalking plus the stigma associated with psychotherapy have precluded the use of mental health services. In addition, victims may face unsympathetic or uninformed police and judges, limited availability of mental health services, and inadequate public funding for counseling services. For example, the 1998 National Violence Against Women Survey (NVAW) found that the police referred only 8% of male and 15% of female stalking targets to victim services (NIJ, 1998, p. 16).

These results parallel research findings that domestic violence victims often do not receive counseling. In a study of an emergency treatment of domestic violence victims, Muelleman and Feighny (1999) reported that only 2% of women who had injuries sought counseling. Brookoff, et al. (1997) found that for domestic violence victims who had called the police previously, only 9% had ever sought counseling (Brookoff, et al., 1997, p. 1371). Muelleman and Feighny (1999) noted that physicians rarely ask about possible domestic violence, and even when they make such a diagnosis, they provide insufficient information to the victims about counseling and other victim services (Muelleman & Feighny, 1999, p. 63).

In some cases, the stalker may have stolen the victim's money so that limited financial resources leave them unable to afford counseling, medical care, and other services. In the Stalking and Violence Project (SVP) Case 45C, Ms. A reported that Mr. B, the father of one of her children, stalked and physically abused her and all of her children (See Appendix B). The perpetrator left her with hundreds of dollars of unpaid utility bills, and because of the lack of money, she had to be put on a waiting list for family counseling.

Victims may be prevented from seeing a therapist because the offenders are monitoring their whereabouts or the burden of work and family responsibilities plus the trauma of stalking make it difficult for stalking targets to obtain help. The severity and duration of the stalking may influence the victims' decision to enter counseling. Persistent threats of death and stalking increase the likelihood that a victim will seek counseling. In SVP Case 18C, Mrs. C was stalked by her husband, Mr. D, and repeatedly told by him that they were going to die soon. At one point, the suspect told her that he was going to kill her and then he would be killed by the police so that they would die together. Mrs. C reported feeling terrified, took anti-depressants, and went into counseling as a result of the trauma caused by her husband's threats and stalking.

The enactment of anti-stalking laws in the United States over the past ten years now makes it possible for stalking victims in certain states to obtain funding for counseling and other services (NIJ, 1993, pp. 36–37). In Montana, a stalker may be required to pay his or her victims for the costs of counseling, medical care, and other services. Likewise, Oregon's anti-stalking law makes it possible for a stalking victim to bring a civil lawsuit against the offender to obtain damages, e.g., the loss of income and the costs of counseling and medical services. The state of Wyoming requires that law enforcement personnel provide emergency services to stalking victims and recommend available victim services.

Treatment for Stalking Victims

Therapists who work with stalking victims find that many have difficulty in trusting other people (Abrams & Robinson, 1998, p. 479).

In order to develop a therapeutic alliance with the client, a clinician must establish a safe and supportive environment wherein the patient begins to understand that he/she bears no responsibility for the stalking and that the onus is strictly on the stalker. To do this, the clinician should tell clients that their therapeutic environment will be safe and supportive (Abrams & Robinson, 1998, p. 479). The therapist needs to understand the social psychology behind client reactions to stalking and avoid creating guilt feelings about the stalker since this can re-traumatize the victim (Abrams & Robinson, 1998, p. 479). No victims consciously seek abuse even when subconscious conflicts or low self-esteem make them vulnerable.

Patients need to learn about the nature and effects of stalking, typical victim responses, legal strategies, and safety and security precautions (Abrams & Robinson, 1998, p. 479; Williams, et al., 1996). This information will help the clients understand their traumatic experiences, minimize their self-doubt, and deal with the trauma. Clinicians should delineate those stalking behaviors that may be indicators of violence. For example, instances in which the offender feels humiliated by the victim's rejection or so-called dramatic moments in offender/victim relationships can increase the stalker's likelihood of committing violence (Meloy, 1997, p. 183).

All patients should be informed that it is normal to have ambivalent feelings toward the stalker as well as feelings of helplessness and resentment toward the inadequacy of the criminal justice system. All this is necessary to keep patients from terminating therapy because of self-blame and fear of rejection by the therapist.

Roberts and Dziegelewski (1996) recommend a crisis intervention approach to treating stalking victims (Roberts & Dziegelewski, 1996, pp. 364–367). This strategy entails five elements. First, the immediate safety needs of the victims need to be addressed. The clinician should determine the psychosocial functioning of the victims as well as the offender's degree of dangerous behavior. Various scales and protocols are available for therapists to establish the victim's initial level of functioning (Roberts & Dziegelewski, 1996, p. 364; Ammerman & Hersen, 1992; Fischer & Corcoran, 1994a; 1994b). Second, the victims need to realize the importance of telling the stalkers that they are no longer interested them and that their behavior is illegal and will not be tolerated. Third, the victim should rehearse this scenario and then actually carry it out, being as direct and specific as possible. Fourth, the stalking target should then end all contact with the perpetrator. Fifth, the therapist should continue to assist the victims during treatment. The clinician should assess for possible dissociative reactions to the stalking, the symptoms related to being a hostage, e.g., the Stockholm Syndrome, suicide, and homicide potential.

Supportive therapy also should focus on assisting the victims in understanding the criminal justice system and how to assert themselves with the police and courts (Abrams & Robinson, 1998, p. 479). Support groups and self-defense programs for stalking victims can help the victims minimize their feelings of isolation, validate their emotional responses to stalking, and share safety and security strategies (Williams, et al., 1996, p. 25). Victim advocates also offer practical and psychological aide to victims.

Severe stalking can result in Post Traumatic Stress Disorder (PTSD), anxiety, depression, and reduced health and social functioning. Miller and Feibelman (1987) point out that in cases of PTSD, the use of anti-anxiety medications under a physician's care can reduce the patients' severe symptoms of anxiety and facilitate their involvement in individual and group psychotherapy (Miller & Feibelman, 1987, pp. 69–73). Moreover, clinicians should be alert to symptoms of anxiety and depression and initiate treatment when warranted.

Therapists may wish to use insight-oriented therapy to aid victims in better understanding their relationships and the cognitive and emotional impact of trauma. However, they should not emphasize these intrapsychic issues exclusively. Instead, therapists should help the patients follow practical security and legal procedures in dealing with the stalker. Clinicians should encourage the victims to call the police and collect detailed information related to the stalking incidents.

Patients should be educated about the available safety and security alternatives. Changing daily routines, relocation to another residence, the use of self-defense techniques, home security systems, and changes in identity are some useful anti-stalking strategies. Victims should be taught to contact the police when needed. These procedures allow the patients to gain control over their trauma even though it may not result in the stalker's arrest.

Clinicians should warn the patients that they may not receive full support from the criminal justice system. This latter point is necessary to emphasize so that the patients do not feel victimized again.

Meloy (1997 & 1999) emphasizes a team-oriented, clinical risk management approach to assist stalking victims. Elements of Meloy's (1997) ten-point strategy include having the victims take personal responsibility for their own safety, documenting the stalker's behaviors, using orders of protection, and involving law enforcement and security investigators. It is also essential to make periodic violence risk assessments based on the perpetrator's history and current relationship with the target (Meloy, 1999, p. 182).

Research on the impact of counseling and therapy on stalking victims is lacking. However, data on the effects of counseling on domestic violence victims at shelters suggest that these services are helpful. According to McNamara, et al. (1997), women who participated in brief counseling and case management services at a domestic shelter reported a reduction in abuse, greater satisfaction with life, improvement in coping skills, and increased satisfaction with shelter services. However, knowledge of long-term outcomes was limited by the shelter's high drop-out rates and lack of follow-up.

Classification and Treatment of Stalkers

It is often difficult to classify stalkers and get them into treatment (Kamphuis & Emmelkamp, 2000, p. 208). Their complex and negative life histories and severe psychiatric diagnoses make it unlikely that they will voluntarily enter therapy. In the United States, courts in several states now require psychiatric or psychological evaluation and treatment of persons convicted of stalking (NIJ, 1993, pp. 29–35, 37). Courts in Alaska require counseling for suspects as a condition of pre-trial release. The courts in Georgia and Michigan require mental health evaluation and counseling as a condition of probation. Illinois, Minnesota, Ohio, and other states also have requirements for mental health evaluation and counseling.

The use of involuntary psychiatric detention and assessment of stalkers may be warranted if it is determined that they have a mental disorder and pose a threat to themselves or others (Williams, et al., 1996, p. 26). In California, this involuntary psychiatric detention initially is for 72 hours, but can be extended to 14 days on the basis of a probable cause hearing and a treating physician's request. Holding the suspect longer than 14 days necessitates a more stringent standard of proof. Persons who have been involuntarily committed are restricted from owning or being in possession of firearms for five years. In addition, the state of California provides for post-arrest diversion of criminal suspects to psychiatric treatment (Williams, et al., 1996, p. 26).

Orders of protection also give victims the opportunity to request assessment and counseling for their offenders. In SVP Case 370C, Ms. E was stalked and assaulted by Mr. F, her former husband. In her order of protection, she asked that Mr. F receive counseling for anger control and alcohol abuse.

It can be very difficult to treat a stalker who enters a program involuntarily. Meloy (1999)'s psychodynamic theory of attachment pathology among stalkers illustrates the problems involved in treating these severely disturbed persons (Meloy, 1999, pp. 87–88). The social context for stalking include chronic failures in relationships, loneliness, major losses, and social isolation. For some of these individuals, emotions such as rage, envy, jealousy, and shame are triggered easily. This is especially true for severely narcissistic persons when desires for attention and control are denied. Rejection then produces shame and humiliation in these offenders, which they defend against with rage toward the self-object (Kohut, 1972). They feel abandoned or disillusioned, which they defend against by reducing the value of the rejecting individual (Meloy, 1999, pp. 88–89). If the target is devalued, then the offender begins to view the victim as being an unworthy object of possession. Stalkers with these emotions will be motivated to follow the victims to injure, control, or kill them.

The most paradoxical aspect of stalking from the psychodynamic perspective is that if the victim is killed, then the stalkers' narcissistic linking fantasy will be reaffirmed. Shakespeare noted this process in Othello, when Othello said: "I will kill thee, and love thee after" (Othello, V, ii 17, 18). This phenomenon also was reflected in a magazine interview with O.J. Simpson, who was accused of stalking and murdering his wife, Nicole Simpson and her friend, Ron Goldman. Simpson reportedly said that if he had murdered his wife, it would have been due to that fact that he loved her very much (Esquire, February 1998, p. 58).

Stalkers have varying life histories, clinical diagnoses, demographic/social profiles, and risks for committing violence. Therefore, their treatment will vary. Since there is a lack of research on the effectiveness of different treatment approaches, there are few guidelines for therapy (Kamphuis & Emmelkamp, 2000, pp. 208–209; Meloy, 1997, p. 180).

Despite the diversity among stalkers, a number of classification guides have been developed to assess their risk for engaging in violence as well as their suitability for treatment and/or incarceration (Mullen, et al., 1999; Zona, et al., 1993 & 1998; Meloy & Gothard, 1995; Harmon, et al., 1995; Roberts & Dziegielewski, 1996). Zona, et al. (1993 & 1998) classified stalkers into three categories: 1) simple obsessional, 2) love obsessional, and 3) erotomanic. More than 50% of all stalkers are in the simple obsessional category. These persons usually stalked sexual partners or persons in non-sexual relationships (Meloy, 1999, pp. 86–87). A majority of these individuals have common mental disorders, such as substance dependence and personality disorders (Meloy, 1997, p. 180).

Palarea, et al. (1999) found that stalkers who had been in sexual relationships with their victims were more likely to commit violence against the victims and their property than those who had not been in intimate relationships (Palarea, et al., 1999, pp. 269–283). In their study, the suspect's proximity and threats toward the victim and their property were positively related to violence, whereas the offender's history of criminal offenses and psychiatric history were not.

In the United Kingdom, Farnham, James and Cantrell (2000) also reported that stalkers who had been in sexually intimate relationships with their victims were more likely to commit serious violence against them than those in non-intimate relationships (Farnham, James & Cantrell, 2000, p. 199). These perpetrators were less likely than those who stalked strangers to have psychotic disorders.

Love obsessional stalkers constitute about 30% of all stalkers (Zona, et al., 1993 & 1998). These persons suffer from a variety of psychiatric problems and frequently involve a man stalking a female acquaintance or stranger. The offender has a fanatical love for the target, and if erotomanic beliefs co-exist, e.g., delusional belief that the target is in love with the stalker when the target does not even know the offender, then these erotomanic beliefs will be secondary to a major mental disorder.

About 10% of stalking cases involve erotomanic offenders who have the delusion that they are loved by a person, when in fact they may be complete strangers. This pathology of unrequited love was first described clinically by Equirol in 1838. In 1921, de Clerambault classified the disorder into two forms: pure and secondary erotomania. The latter type is superimposed on a pre-existing paranoid disorder. Once thought to be a rare disorder that mainly afflicted women who stalked higher status men, these cases now are fairly common and occur among men and women (Dietz, et al., 1991a; Dietz, et al., 1991b; Meloy, 1992, pp. 21–22). The duration of stalking among erotomanics is the longest of the three types of stalkers and the risk of violence is the lowest (less than 5% of erotomanic persons are violent) (Meloy, 1992, pp. 21–22).

There have been a number of well-known stalking cases (Meloy, 1992, pp. 21–22; Caplan, 1987; Tarasoff v. Regents of the University of California, 1976; Blum, 1986). The stalking and murder of Tatiana Tarasoff by Prosenjit Poddar resulted in changes in the scope of psychotherapy (Tarasoff v. Regents of the University of California, 1976). Another noteworthy example was John Hinckley, Jr.'s attempted assassination of President Ronald Reagan after his stalking of actress Jodie Foster. Before the shooting, Hinckley wrote a note to the actress, saying that he would not shoot President Reagan if he could win her heart and be with her for the rest of his life (Caplan, 1987, p. 21). Robert John Bardo's stalking and murder of actress Rebecca Schaeffer on July 18, 1989, led to the enactment of the first anti-stalking law in California (Meloy, 1992, p. 22). Other stalking victims have included Madonna, comedian David Letterman, and tennis star Martina Hingis.

Zona, et al. (1993, 1998) found that about 2% of stalking cases involve false allegations of being victimized. Likewise, Pathe, et al. (1999) found evidence of some false claims of victimization. False victims frequently have a personality disorder that may be based on conscious, subconscious, or delusional processes (Zona, et al., 1993 & 1998). Individuals may make false accusations because they have a secondary gain, e.g., winning in child custody cases.

Mullen, et al. (1999) categorized stalkers into five groups based on the context of the stalking and the offender's motivation

(Mullen, 1999, p. 1246): (1) rejected, (2) intimacy seeking, (3) incompetent, (4) resentful, and (5) predatory stalkers. For rejected stalkers, stalking can be a response to being rejected. These individuals experience feelings of loss, frustration, anger, jealousy, and vindictiveness. Many stalkers who have been rejected have personality disorders, although some have delusional disorders, including morbid jealousy.

In SVP Case 337, the perpetrator exhibited a variety of these emotions, including feelings of abandonment, anger, and vindictiveness. Ms. G, a single parent of an 18-year-old, had been living with her partner, Ms. H, for over $2\frac{1}{2}$ years. One day as Ms. G was leaving their residence to go to work, the offender became very agitated and begged her: "Don't leave me, don't abandon me." Ms. H refused to let Ms. G go to work alone. While the victim was driving her car, the offender, who was sitting in the passenger side, grabbed the steering wheel and tried to steer the car into a wall. Ms. H also stole her computer, smashed her telephone, and tried to steal money out of their joint bank account.

Intimacy-seeking offenders stalk as a way of gaining intimacy with people whom they perceive as their true love even though they may be strangers (Mullen, et al., 1999, p. 1246). These perpetrators can have erotomanic delusions and believe that their love is mutual. Other stalkers of this type may suffer from schizophrenia and mania, morbid infatuation, and personality disorders. Some intimacy-seeking stalkers become jealous and may become enraged over their target's rejection.

Incompetent stalkers know that their targets do not love them but continue to stalk their targets because they hope that their stalking will lead to intimacy. These stalkers include people who have limited social and intellectual functioning and little knowledge of courtship rituals. They have a sense of entitlement to their target and are unable or unwilling to begin with a non-intimate form of a relationship. These persons frequently have stalked other targets. The incompetent stalkers view their targets as attractive partners but do not give them special qualities.

Resentful stalkers seek to scare and harass their targets. Some stalk their victims because they have vendettas against them, while others select their targets at random and stalk them because of a general feeling of grievance. One man stalked a physician because he thought the clinician had failed to diagnose his wife's cervical cancer. Another perpetrator recently had an humiliating experience and began to stalk a female stranger whom he saw on the street, simply because she appeared to be attractive, happy, and successful.

Predatory stalkers are sexual predators and stalking gives them a sense of power. They familiarize themselves with the victims' routines and fantasize about their future attacks. Stalking continues over a long time before they attack their victims or are arrested. One male predatory stalker obtained help after planning to abduct and rape his victim in an isolated house, which he had equipped to carry out his crimes. Most predatory stalkers have sexual perversions and are more likely than other stalker types to have a history of sexual offense convictions.

Mullen, et al. (1999) reported that intimacy-seeking stalkers need assertive therapy since they do not respond well to criminal justice penalties (Mullen, et al., 1999, p. 1248). They may view court appearances and incarceration as the "price of true love." In contrast, rejected stalkers, except for those in child custody disputes and morbidly jealous persons, may be amenable to judicial intervention. Incompetent stalkers can be persuaded to stop their stalking, but then they easily find another target. Resentful stalkers who are often are self-righteous, are fairly impervious to therapy, and criminal justice intervention can increase their feelings of injustice and exacerbate related stalking behaviors. Criminal justice efforts should emphasize apprehending predatory stalkers since they focus on planning and carrying out sexual offenses.

Another category of stalker is the controlling stalker who uses stalking as part of a repertoire of behaviors to control his victim. They may establish special rules for that person's behavior and determine whom they can befriend. Stalking can help perpetrators control their victims by enabling them to monitor their actions and thus ensure that they are following the rules. In SVP Case 428SF, Ms. L was stalked, physically abused, and raped by her husband, Mr. M. The perpetrator was very controlling. He deprived his wife of food and money unless she followed his orders and refused to help her complete her immigration papers.

Those stalkers with major mental disorders are difficult to treat. Psychotherapy, medications, and general support are needed for these offenders. Although stalkers with personality disorders are a diverse group, many can be effectively managed with training in social skills and psychotherapy.

However, Meloy (1997) suggests that the prognosis is generally poor for stalkers who are motivated mainly by antisocial and paranoid disorders and abandonment rage (Meloy, 1997, p. 180). Aggressive prosecution of this type of offender and their segregation from the victim is desirable since there is no current effective treatment.

Similarly, erotomanic or psychotic persons tend to be very resistant to treatment (Kamphuis & Emmelkamp, 2000, p. 208). In contrast, offenders with delusional mental disorders may find that medication may eliminate their fixed and false beliefs (Meloy, 1997, p. 180).

According to Kamphuis and Emmelkamp (2000), interventions for stalkers with severe personality disorders should combine both legal and treatment approaches (Kamphuis & Emmelkamp, 2000, p. 208). Meloy (1997) also argues that both humane treatment and incarceration are necessary (Meloy, 1997, p. 181). Stalking targets must be protected from the offenders. Furthermore, the stalkers need to realize that their behaviors are illegal and that therapy is available to them. The need for both mental health and criminal justice responses was incorporated into California's anti-stalking law. That law required the courts to consider psychiatric treatment and possible institutionalization for the offenders.

Segregation, Incarceration, and Monitoring of Stalkers

Segregation and incarceration of perpetrators may help to protect the victim from further stalking. Incarceration, however, can be ineffective. Often the perpetrator is arrested for a very short time period and soon is back on the street (Abrams & Robinson, 1998, p. 478). In some cases, the offender is further incensed by their arrest and imprisonment and will intensify their stalking and related violence once they are released.

Incarcerated offenders can continue stalking their victims from prison (Meloy, 1997, p. 181). For example, Arthur Jackson, who was diagnosed as having paranoid schizophrenia, continued to harass Hollywood actress Theresa Saldana even after he was imprisoned (Meloy, 1997, p. 181).

Imprisonment can fulfill offenders' desire for notoriety. In the case of Robert Hoskins, incarceration transformed his narcissistic fantasies into reality. Hoskins painted "Madonna Love Me" and "The Madonna Stalker" on his prison wall. Additional charges could be brought against these inmates to assist parole boards in deciding if they are ready to be released. A collaboration of prison officials, prosecutors, and security personnel might help protect the victim from further harm.

Stalking victims face additional trauma and can re-experience their stalker's psychological control when they are required to testify against the suspect in open court. The celebrity, Madonna, who was stalked by Robert Hoskins, stated that her testimony in court made her stalker's fantasies come true since she was sitting in front of him in the court room (Meloy, 1997, p. 178).

Electronic monitoring, which has been used to monitor sex offenders, also has been used to keep stalkers away from their victims. In the United States, the courts in certain states require electronic monitoring as a condition of pre-trial release or probation or as alternative to incarceration (NIJ, 1993, p. 36). Electronic monitoring is becoming popular in other countries as well. The United Kingdom is planning the use of new electronic tags in anti-stalking and other cases (Travis, "Straw plans new tags for stalkers and sex offenders," The Guardian, March 13, 2000; "Sex criminals may be tagged," BBC Homepage, March 16, 2000). These tags, instead of being activated when the offender leaves home during a curfew, will have alarms that are triggered if the perpetrator approaches the victim's home.

Conclusion

With the new public recognition of stalking as a social and legal problem, there is increased interest in counseling and therapy for both victims and perpetrators (Lowney & Best, 1995, pp. 33–57). Mental health interventions can help victims gain needed crisis intervention skills. Likewise, treatment and long-term incarceration can help to control stalkers' undesirable behaviors. Studies of the short-term and long-term effects of segregation and incarceration of offenders are needed. The impact of treatment on stalking victims also should be investigated.

Conclusion

This book offers a review of the literature plus a report of new research on the problem of stalking and its impact on society. First, stalking is an old problem that still continues to occur in a variety of relationships. According to the Stalking and Violence Project (SVP), 28% of the victims who filed orders of protection reported being stalked by intimate partners, relatives, and acquaintances. These results are higher than the prevalence of stalking in the National Violence Against Women Survey (NVAW), which estimated that 1% of women and 0.4% of men are stalked each year. The prevalence rate was higher in the SVP because it was based on a subset of the population, e.g., those who have filed protective orders, instead of a random sample of the general population However, the NVAW study also indicates that this is still a problem that many women and men face each year. For both conflict-oriented and stable relationships and acquaintances, stalking can be used to establish, maintain, and terminate relationships.

Second, some people use stalking as a means to achieve power and exert control in their every day relationships. Thus, stalking provides an emotional release to relieve feelings of jealousy and anger and attain specific goals. Stalking that results from anger and jealousy is more likely to result in physical violence and trauma for the victims than stalking that is motivated by other concerns. This was corroborated by the SVP, where stalkers with a history of violence were more likely than other stalkers to use violence.

Third, certain characteristics of relationships will facilitate or inhibit stalking. In dating relationships, the offenders use stalking to form new relationships, maintain existing ones, and retaliate against their dates for terminating their dating relationships. In contrast, spouses use stalking to maintain relationships as well as gain the upper hand in family disputes.

Fourth, stalking of short duration and low severity may result in the targets not perceiving the behaviors as stalking. Some victims also may deny the existence of stalking because they fear that the perpetrator will become violent. Other victims may be stigmatized and embarrassed about being stalked.

Fifth, factors such as gender, age, and ethnicity of the victims and perpetrators seem to influence the initiation and maintenance of stalking and violence. For instance, the SVP found that younger persons were more likely to engage in stalking behaviors and violence than older persons. Gender also influences patterns of stalking. Both the NVAW and the SVP found that women were more likely to be stalked than men. Other factors such as pregnancy inhibit the onset of stalking behaviors.

Sixth, the stress and trauma of stalking is exacerbated by the ineffectiveness of the criminal justice system in dealing with stalking incidents. Many stalking victims develop stress-related health problems, anxiety, depression, and Post Traumatic Stress Disorder, and need to obtain counseling.

Seventh, the social and demographic characteristics and the type of offender behaviors seem to affect the manner in which police assistance is sought. The NVAW reported that the police were more likely to arrest or detain a suspect if female victims were involved than if there were male victims involved. In the SVP, stalking victims involved in police contacts were more likely to have been recipients of serious violence who sustained physical and emotional trauma.

Eighth, social change has impacted face-to-face relations. With media coverage of highly publicized cases of stalking and increased awareness of Internet stalking, private experiences have become transformed into public dilemmas. Stalking targets now understand their predicament is not unique but they share a similar plight with others. As a result, stalking victims in increasing numbers are asking for help by contacting the police, courts, and social and psychological services.

Ninth, technological change has opened new avenues for stalkers, e.g., e-mail and fax machines. Electronic chat rooms provide a vehicle for stalkers to exploit not only their victims, but may serve as recruiting territory for new targets.

Tenth, the awareness of stalking as a social problem has led to new organizational responses to stalking. Legislators, in response to public pressure, enacted anti-stalking laws. The federal government developed the Model Anti-Stalking Code to assist local and state law enforcement, and federal anti-stalking laws were passed to strengthen law enforcement efforts. The National Violence Against Women Act was passed to aid in the coordination of law enforcement efforts and community groups in combating violence and stalking against women. Many community-based and Internet-based groups also were established to oppose stalking, while other groups sprang up to oppose anti-stalking laws on the grounds that they threatened constitutional rights to free speech and other protected rights.

We have just begun to understand the phenomenon of stalking, and much research needs to be done. What is the future of stalking research? Much work needs to be done to answer a variety of questions, including: What is the prevalence of stalking in different relationships? Who is at risk of stalking? Is it possible to develop profiles of dangerous stalkers? To what degree is socioeconomic status related to stalking? What is the relationship between stalking and violence? What factors increase or lessen the probability of stalking and violence in different relationships?

How effective is psychotherapy in helping victims and rehabilitating perpetrators? What are the long-term effects of the use of the criminal justice system and incarceration on the victims and suspects?

Society needs new information on how to cope with stalkers and effectively help their victims. The criminal justice system, legislators, and the mental health profession need accurate information on appropriate strategies for dealing with these traumatic and dangerous behaviors.

Appendix A

Research Methods

Since the advent of anti-stalking laws, stalking victims in some domestic courts are now given an opportunity to formally complain about stalking incidents and request court protection against stalking. A new interpersonal stalking protocol was constructed to code self-report data on stalking and violence based on newly filed domestic orders of protection.

Sample

A random sample of 519 newly filed domestic orders of protection (also known as restraining orders or protective orders) was drawn from new domestic court case listings that were published in legal newspapers in two cities (Midwest and West regions) between 1997 and 1999. The sample of domestic orders of protection consisted of 519 self-reported victims and 519 accused persons.

Measures

An interpersonal stalking protocol was constructed to code self-report data obtained from a content analysis of the newly filed domestic orders of protection. The protocol was pre-tested using 25 randomly selected new domestic orders of protection. The final stalking protocol consisted of 154 variables.

One section of the protocol consisted of 29 residential, demographic, and family variables and 20 census tract measures of socioeconomic status for both the self-reported victims and accused individuals. The self-reported victims are the persons who are filing orders of protection to bar the accused persons from contacting them. Socioeconomic status variables for both victims and accused persons could be coded directly from the orders of protection. Therefore, 20 census tract measures of socioeconomic status for both victims and accused individuals were obtained by matching known residential addresses of victims and accused persons with the 1990 U.S. Census Bureau Census Tract database.

Information about the incidents or problems that led the alleged victims to file orders of protection against the accused persons is contained in the second part of the protocol. This section contains 89 variables concerning the type of relationship between the victims and the accused individuals, the victims' self-report narrative of what reportedly transpired, and the victims' reasons for filing the orders of protection.

Three stalking variables were constructed from the victims' self-report narratives. If the victims' narratives contained allegations that the accused individuals followed or stalked them, kept them under surveillance, or lay in wait for them, then these behaviors were coded as positive for the first stalking variable, "stalking." Before filing the orders of protection, victims were notified that stalking is illegal. The first stalking variable under-reports stalking since it may not include other behaviors such as receiving unwanted telephone calls and letters at home and at work that also are considered part of the stalking phenomenon. Thus, this variable only measures the victims' perception of stalking as a following or surveillance phenomenon.

The second stalking variable, "multiple stalking," was constructed to be as comprehensive as possible. If the victims' narratives contained allegations about any type of repeated and unwanted communication and intrusion, e.g., threatening the victims in their homes or at work and making threatening calls to the victims at work, then the data were coded on a scale from 1 (one form of stalking) to 7 (seven forms of stalking).

The third stalking variable, "stalking distance," was constructed based on data from the multiple stalking variable. The stalking distance variable measures the proximity of stalkers to the victims.

Alleged perpetrators who stalked victims were ranked on a scale from 1 (sending a letter—least close) to 7 (being followed—most close). The stalking distance variable, like the multiple stalking variable, does not rely on the victims' perception of stalking.

The last section of the interpersonal stalking protocol consists of 16 variables related to the self-reported victims' request for domestic court protection and the courts' approval or disapproval of their requests. Victims indicated whether they sought court protection for a variety of complaints, including physical abuse, stalking, and intimidation of dependents. This section also contains information on whether the court approved the victims' request for court protection in these specific problem areas.

Demographic and Socioeconomic Status of the Sample

Table 1 contains selected data on the demographic and socioeconomic status characteristics of the victims of all forms of domestic violence and stalking. Eighty-three percent of the self-reported

Table 1. Sample Characteristics of the Victims of Stalking and Other Forms of Violence (N = 519)

Gender: Females—83% Males—17%
(Chi-Square = 219.67, df = 1, p < .000)

Racial/Ethnic Background:
White—21%
African-American—56%
Hispanic—20%
Asian and Other—3%
(Chi-Square = 449.67, df = 4, p < .000)
Age: (unknown)

Marital Status: Married—67%
(Chi-Square = 101.43, df = 1, p < .000)

Dating Status: Dating—26%
(Chi-Square = 116.10, df = 1, p < .000)

Parents of at Least One Child—53%
(Chi-Square = 45.18, df = 1, p < .000)

% Living in Census Tracts
With a Median Income:
40% <$20,000
50% $20,000–$39,999
9% $40,000–$59,999
1% $60,000–$79,999
(Chi-Square = 335.72, df = 3, p < .000)

victims in the sample were female and 17% male. Sixty-seven percent of the victims in the sample reported that they were married to the accused persons, 2% indicated they were formerly married to the accused individuals, 9% formerly lived with the accused persons, 3% reported currently living with the accused persons, 26% indicated that they were dating or have dated the accused individuals, and 8% reported being a relative of the accused persons. Fifty-three percent of the victims indicated that they were the parents of at least one child. Of these victims, 46% reported having 1 child, 40% had 2–3 children and 9% reported having 4 or more children.

Forty-one percent of the victims lived in census tracts with less than 20% Whites (Chi-Square = 138.06, df = 4, p < .000, N = 498), 48% of the victims lived in census tracts with less than 20% African-Americans (Chi-Square = 314.03, df = 4, p < .000, N = 498), and 72% of the victims lived in census tracts with less than 20% Hispanics (Chi-Square = 864.74, df = 4, p < .000, N = 497).

Forty percent of the victims in the sample resided in census tracts with a median income of less than $20,000, and 50% of the victims resided in census tracts with median income between $20,000 and 39,999. Only 9% of the victims in the sample lived in census tracts with a median income between $40,000 and $59,999, and 1% lived in census tracts with a median income between $60,000 and $79,999.

Information on the sample of individuals accused of all forms of domestic violence and stalking are presented in Table 2. In regard to the characteristics of the accused individuals, 80% were male and 20% were female. Sixteen percent of the accused were between 18 and 25 years old, 53% were in the 26–40 age group, 23% were in the 41–60 age group, and 2% were over the age of 60. In regard to accused persons' ethnic and racial characteristics, 21% were White, 53% were African-American, and 20% were Hispanic. Three percent of the alleged offenders were Asian and one percent were members of other ethnic and racial groups. Because of the limited numbers in these two latter groups, they were not used in subsequent analysis. Forty percent of the alleged perpetrators lived in census tracts with a median income of less than $20,000, 52% resided in census tracts with a median income between $20,000 and $39,999, and 7% lived in census tracts with a median income between $40,000 and $59,999.

Table 2. Sample Characteristics of the Individuals Accused
of Stalking and Other Forms of Violence (N = 519)

Gender: Females—20% Males—80%
(Chi-Square = 219.67, df = 1, p < .000)

Racial/Ethnic Background:
White—22%
African-American—54%
Hispanic—21%
Asian and Other—3%

Age:
18–25 years of age—17%
26–40 years of age—57%
41–60 years of age—24%
60 years of age—2%

Marital Status: Married—67%
(Chi-Square = 101.43, df = 1, p < .000)

Dating Status: Dating—26%
(Chi-Square = 116.10, df = 1, p < .000)

% Living in Census Tracts
With a Median Income:
40% < $20,000
52% $20,000–$39,999
7% $40,000–$59,999
1% $60,000–$79,999
(Chi-Square = 322.44, df = 3, p < .000)

Accused Whites, African-Americans, and Hispanics differed significantly in terms of their census tract-based median income (Chi-Square = 78.50, df = 12, p < .000, N = 422). As in the case of the self-reported victims, alleged Hispanic perpetrators lived in census tracts with the lowest median income. Sixty-three percent of the accused Hispanics lived in census tracts with a median income less than $20,000, compared to 24% of the accused African-Americans and 6% of the accused Whites. Seventy-four percent of the alleged White perpetrators and 48% of the accused African-Americans resided in census tracts with a median income between $20,000 and $39,999.

Demographics of the Stalking Victims and Accused Stalkers

Table 3 contains data on the demographic and socioeconomic characteristics of the stalking victims. Twenty-eight percent of the victims in the sample reported that they had been stalked by the accused. Eighty-two percent of the victims who reported being stalked were female and 18% were male. Thirty-six percent of those alleging that they were stalked had dated or were currently dating the accused persons. Of those victims who claimed that they were being stalked, 53% were parents of at least one child.

Fifty-three percent of the stalking victims lived in census tracts with a median income between $20,000 and $39,999, 37% resided in census tracts with a median income less than $20,000, and 9% lived in census tracts with a median income of $40,000 or more (Chi-Square = 99.75, df = 3, p < .000, N = 145, Table 3).

Table 4 shows the demographic and socioeconomic character-istics of the accused stalkers. With regard to the background of the alleged stalkers, 82% were male and 18% were female. Twenty-five

Table 3. Demographic/Socioeconomic Status Characteristics of the Stalking Victims (N=145)

Gender: Females—82% Males—18%
(Chi-Square = 61.40, df = 1, p < .000)

Racial/Ethnic Background:
White—23%
African-American—53%
Hispanic—21%
Asian and Others—3%
(Chi-Square = 64.32, df = 3, p < .000)

Age: (unknown)

Marital Status: Married—25%
(Chi-Square = 38.27, df= 1, p < .000)
Dating Status: Dating—36%
(Chi-Square = 11.44, df= 1, p < .001)
Parents of at Least One Child—53%
(Chi-Square = 58.84, df= 1, p < .000)

% Living in Census Tracts
With a Median Income:
37% < $20,000
53% $20,000–$39,999
8% $40,000–$59,999
1% $60,000–$79,999
(Chi-Square = 99.75, df = 3, p < .000)

28% of the Victims Reported Being Stalked
(Chi-Square = 97.54, df = 1, p < .000)

Table 4. Demographic/Socioeconomic Status Characteristics of the
Accused Stalkers (N = 145)

Gender: Females—18% Males—82%

Racial/Ethnic Background:
White-25%
African-American—51%
Hispanic—19%
Asian and Others—5%
(Chi-Square = 64.79, df= 3, p < .000)

Age:
18–25 years of age—14%
26–40 years of age—60%
41–60 years of age—25%
1% > 60—1%
(Chi-Square = 106.29, df= 3, p < .000)

Marital Status: Married—25%
(Chi-Square = 38.27, df= 1, p < .000)

Dating Status: Dating—36%
(Chi-Square = 11.44, df= 1, p < .001)

% Living in Census Tracts
With a Median Income:
45% < $20,000
50% $20,000–$39,999
5% $40,000–$59,999
(Chi-Square = 89.47, df= 3, p < .000)

percent of the accused stalkers were White, 51% were African-American, and 19% were Hispanics.

In terms of the age of the accused stalkers, 14% were in the 18–25 age group, 59% were ages 26 to 40, 26% were ages 41 to 60, and 1% were over 60 years of age. Forty-five percent of the alleged stalkers lived in census tracts with a median income less than $20,000 and 50% resided in census tracts with a median income between $20,000 and $39,999. The ethnic/racial background of the accused offenders was not related to their census tract median incomes. However, the trends were similar to the relationship between the racial/ethnic background of stalking victims and the census tract median incomes of stalking victims. For example, 60% of the alleged Hispanic stalkers resided in census tract with a median income less than $20,000, compared to 28% of the accused African-American stalkers and 6% of the accused White stalkers.

Appendix B

Selected Cases from the Stalking and Violence Project

Intimate Partner Stalking

SVP Case 45C shows how stalking, threats, and harassment can occur after the break up of a non-married couple who had lived together. In addition, this case shows that threats of child kidnapping are made in the context of former intimate stalking and harassment. Ms. S stated that her former intimate partner, Mr. T, a 33-year-old male, frequently comes to her home uninvited and refuses to leave. Mr. T is physically and verbally abusive to her and her children. The offender has threatened to kidnap Ms. S's children and kill her. After the break-up of their relationship, he had left Ms. S with hundreds of dollars of unpaid utility bills. As a result, she has had to rely on food pantries. Ms. S has filed three police reports against the offender and is afraid that he will harm her and her children. Because of the stresses associated with his stalking, threats, and harassment, she has applied for family counseling and is on a waiting list.

In SVP Case 467SF, Ms. E, who had lived with Mr. F, was assaulted by him after ending their relationship. Mr. F grabbed her, slammed her against a wall, and spit on her. It was only later, after

Mr. F broke into her home, stole her computer and other personal items, and tapped her phone line that Ms. E called the police.

In SVP Case 478SF, Ms. L had been in a lesbian relationship with Ms. M, whom she had met through a personal ad. Ms. M threatened to commit suicide if Ms. L broke up the relationship, and Ms. M drove recklessly with her in the car. The victim filed two police reports against the offender.

Family and Relative Stalking

SVP Case 278C shows how family and relative stalking can cause severe stress for the victim. Ms. W complained that her brother, Mr. X, a 38-year-old man, had stalked her and threatened to kill her several times. The sister had asked her brother to move out of their house so that another brother of hers who was visiting from Puerto Rico could stay with her. Mr. X became angry with his sister because he thought that she was kicking him out of the house. He telephoned his sister and threatened to kill her because she had thrown him out of the house. He also threatened to have his gang "get her." Ms. W reported that she was unable to sleep because she was afraid that her brother, Mr. X, would come to her home and follow through with his threats to kill her.

SVP Case 489SF involved a niece/aunt relationship. Ms. M, a single, 26-year-old niece, was accused of stalking, threatening, and attempting to assault her aunt, Ms. N. The aunt claimed that Ms. M made several death threats over the phone, was verbally abusive, tried to hit her, and had her boyfriend drive around her residence. They had a history of disputes over the niece's illicit drug use and welfare status. Ms. M was previously arrested and jailed for illegal drug use and her husband is currently in jail for drug use.

Stalking in a Dating Relationship

SVP Case 165C illustrates stalking, harassment, and vandalism against a woman who had been in a dating relationship with another woman. Ms. K accused Ms. L, a 42-year-old single woman, of stalking her repeatedly, making unwanted telephone calls to her at home and work, leaving letters for her at her workplace, and slashing and deflating her car tires. The victim had begun a new relationship, and it seemed that jealousy was a motivating factor in Ms. L's actions.

SVP Case 340C is an example of a stalker, Mr. Q, a single 49-year-old man, who has pursued and threatened to kill a woman whom he had been dating, Ms. R and her children. The offender threatened the victim and her children with a dagger, but did not physically attack them. Ms. R asserted that the perpetrator followed her "all of the time." For example, he follows her when she takes her children to school and then stays and watches them.

In SVP Case 222C, Mr. S, a single 24-year-old man, stalked Ms. T, whom he had been dating, and vandalized her automobile. The victim claimed that the perpetrator has pursued her at home various times and "jumped" on her several times one day. One time, while Mr. S was stalking the victim, he made several dents in her car. In addition, Ms. T charged that Mr. S had knocked out the windows in her grandmother's house.

In SVP Case 218C, a female victim, Ms. J, who had been dating Mr. K, had been assaulted several times, was threatened with a knife, and almost run over by Mr. K. He made harassing calls, showed up unannounced at her home, and stole items from her home. After he stole personal belongings from her home, Ms. J filed a police report.

Stalking in Marital Relationships

SVP Case 227C is an example of an offender, Mr. Y, a 33-year-old man, who pursued his wife, Mrs. Z, and vandalized her property. The perpetrator rang Mrs. Z's doorbell at 2:30 in the morning and repeatedly telephoned her. One day, Mr. Y threatened to "blow up" her house. The next day, he broke into a first floor window of her home. The wife noted that her husband uses cocaine in excess. To avoid her husband, Mrs. Z and her 9-year-old daughter moved to a friend's house.

Jealousy as a Motivation for Stalking

Other cases in the SVP illustrate jealousy among stalkers who are current or past cohabiting couples or in dating relationships.

In SVP Case 121, Ms. J, who had been in a dating relationship with Mr. K., was told by the offender that he would kill her if he saw her with someone else. A year later, Ms. J was driving her car when she noticed that Mr. K was following her. She was unsuccessful in evading him. When Ms. J got out of her car, the perpetrator came up to her and told her that he would find out where she lived.

The Impact of Stalking

Other SVP cases showed that the severe stresses of stalking worsened the victim's pre-existing health problems. In SVP Case #422, Ms. N, stated that Mr. O, whom she had been dating, stalked and abused her sexually, physically, and emotionally. After being punched unconscious, Ms. N is now terrified and afraid for her life and her daughter's life. Ms. N had been an incest survivor and in therapy for this abuse. Her condition has worsened because of the physical abuse, and she is now in therapy for the current physical abuse.

SVP Case 208C shows that a victim developed a new medical problem, high blood pressure, as a result of persistent stalking, threatening behaviors, vandalism, and thefts by Ms. Q, whom he had been dating.

SVP Case 211C shows the effects of spouse stalking and abuse on both the wife and daughter. In addition to stalking his wife and daughter, Mr. S choked and stomped on his wife, Mrs. T. Their daughter was too afraid to go to school because of her father's stalking and attack on her mother, and Mrs. T was too afraid to leave home to escort her daughter and son to school.

About 1% of the stalking targets in the SVP study reportedly left their job or school. SVP Case 101C, which was previously discussed, illustrates a situation where the stalking victim left her job to escape the stalker. Ms. A was harassed and stalked for a period of four years by Mr. B. After Ms. A told Mr. B that she was not interested in becoming more romantically involved, she was stalked by the offender. Late one night during the first year of her victimization, Ms. A stated that her phone rang almost continuously and that her outside apartment buzzer rang for minutes at a time. The victim complained to her university but felt this did not stop the offender from harassing and stalking her. Finally, she quit her on-campus library job to avoid having any contact with the stalker.

Stalking Victims Seek Medical Care

SVP Case 37C describes a situation in which a stalking victim obtained emergency medical care for domestic violence-related injuries. Ms. I repeatedly had been physically abuse and had her car vandalized by Mr. J, whom she had been dating. One day, Ms. I was driving her car and realized that Mr. J was following her in another car. She pulled over at a nearby gas station and the perpetrator got into her car and asked why she had called the police about him a few days earlier. Ms. I told him to get out of the car, and he responded by biting her nose and pulling her hair. The offender's bite left visible indentations on her nose. She filed a police report and went to the hospital emergency room, where she received medical treatment for a human bite.

Stalking Victims and Police Assistance

SVP Case 249C consisted of a spouse victim who was involved in police intervention. Mrs. C was told by her husband, Mr. D, that he was going to get a divorce so that her immigration papers would be rejected. Later that day, he and several of his cousins assaulted her. He slammed a door into her hand and broke one of her fingers. He then grabbed his wife by her hair and hit her head on the door. Mrs. C was able to escape and run from him. Her son called the police, and they arrested the offender and took the victim to the hospital.

In SVP Case 337C, Ms. N, a single parent of an adult child, previously had shared a residence with Ms. O, her partner. The offender previously had verbally and physically abused Ms. N many times in the past. However, it was not until Ms. N found that Ms. O had stolen her computer and smashed her telephones that she filed a report with the police.

References

Abrams, K.M. & Robinson, G.E. (1998). Stalking part II: Victims' problems with the legal system and therapeutic considerations. *Canadian Journal of Psychiatry, 43* (5): 477–481.

American Civil Liberties Union v. Reno, 31 F.Supp. 2d 473, 476, 493 (E.D. Pa. 1999).

Ammerman, R.T. & Hersen, M. (Eds.) (1992). *Assessment of family violence: A clinical and legal sourcebook.* New York: Wiley.

Blum, D. (1986). Bad karma: A true story of obsession and murder. New York: Atheneum.

Boychuk, M. Katherine (1994). Are stalking laws unconstitutionally vague or overbroad? *Northwestern University Law Review, 88* (2), 769–802.

Brewster, Mary P. (2000). Stalking by former intimates: verbal threats and other predictors of physical violence. *Violence and Victims, 15* (1), 41–54.

Brookoff, D., et al. (1997). Characteristics of participants in domestic violence-Assessment at the scene of domestic assault. *Journal of the American Medical Association, 277* (17), 1369–1373.

Burgess, A.W., Baker, T., Greening, D., et al. (1997). Stalking behaviors within domestic violence. *Journal of Family Violence, 12* (4), 389–403.

Caplan, L. (1987). The *insanity defense and the trial of John W. Hinckley, Jr.* New York: Dell.

Channel, 3000, January 22, 1999, pp. 1–2.

Chicago Tribune, May 27, 1994.

Chicago Tribune, July 6, 1997.

Chicago Tribune, September 27, 1992 at C4.

Chicago Tribune, September 30, 1992 at C5.

CNN.com, 2000, pp. 1–2.

CNN.com, May 9, 2000, pp. 1–2.

Conn. Gen. Stat. Ann. 53a–181c, West Supp. 1993.

Cupach, W. R. & Spitzberg, B. H. (1998). Obsessive relational intrusion and stalking. In B. H. Spitzberg & W. R. Cupach (Eds.), *The dark side of close relationships* (pp. 233–263). Mahwah, N.J.: L Erlbaum.

www.cyberangels.org

CyberSpace Law Center, http://cyber.lp.findlaw.com

The Dallas Morning News, 10-15-96.

de Clerambault, C.G. (1921). Les psychoses passionelles (pp. 315–322). In *Oeuvres Psychiatriques.* Paris: Universitaires de France, 1942.

Dietz, P.E. (1984). A remedial approach to harassment. *Virginia Law Review* (70), 507–544.

Dietz, P., et al. (1991a). Threatening and otherwise inappropriate letters to Hollywood celebrities. *Journal of Forensic Sciences, 36,* 185–209.

Dietz, P., et al. (1991b). Threatening and otherwise inappropriate letters to members of the Unites States Congress. *Journal of Forensic Sciences, 36,* 1445–1468.

Eigenberg, H. & Moriarty, L. (1991). Domestic violence and local law enforcement in Texas: Examining police officers' awareness of state legislation. *Journal of Interpersonal Violence*, 6, 102–109.

Elder, Salon Media, Dec. 12, 1999, pp. 1–3.

Elliott, D.S. (1994). Serious violent offenders: onset, developmental course, and termination—The American Society of Criminology 1993 Presidential Address. *Criminology, 32* (1), 1–21.

Emerson, R.M., Ferris, K.O., Gardner, C.B. et al. (1998). On being stalked. *Social Problems, 45*, 289–314.

Esquirol, J.E.D. (1838). Mental Maladies: *A Treatise on Insanity*. Trans. E.K. Hunt, New York: Hafner, 1965.

Fain, Constance F. (1981). Conjugal violence: legal and psychosociological remedies *Syracuse Law Review, 32*, 497, 562.

Farnham, F.R., James, D.V., & Cantrell, P. (2000). Association between violence, psychosis, and relationship to victim in stalkers. *Lancet, 355*, 199.

Fernandez-Esquer, M. & McCloskey, L. (1999). Coping with partner abuse among Mexican-American and Anglo Women: Ethnic and socioeconomic influences. *Violence and Victims, 14* (3), 293–310.

Fischer, J. & Corcoran, K. (1994a). *Measures for clinical practice: A source book. Vol. 1: Couples, Families and Children* (2nd ed.)., New York: Free Press.

Fischer, J. & Corcoran, K. (1994b). *Measures for clinical practice: A source book. Vol. 2: Adults* (2nd ed.)., New York: Free Press.

Fla. Stat. Ann. 784.048 (5) West (1992).

Fleury, R.E., Sullivan, C.M., Bybee, D.I., & Davidson, W.S. (1998). Why don't they just call the cops?: Reasons for differential police contact among women with abusive partners. *Violence and Victims, 13* (4), 333–346.

Fountain, J.W. & Kirby, J. (1992). *Chicago Tribune*, August 5, p. D1.

Fremouw, W. J., Westrup, D., & Pennypacker, J. (1997). Stalking on campus: The prevalence and strategies for coping with stalking. *Journal of Forensic Sciences, 42*, 664–667.

Glod, Infowar.com, April 14, 2000, pp. 1–5.

Godwin, M., Cyberstalking, www.investigativepsych.com, pp. 1–2.

www.gseis.ucla.edu

Hall, D. M. (1998). The victims of stalking. In J.R. Meloy (Ed.), *The psychology of stalking: Clinical and forensic perspectives*. San Diego: Academic Press.

Hall, D. (1996). Outside looking in: Stalkers and their victims. Paper presented at the Academy of Criminal Justice Sciences Conference, San Francisco, CA.

Hamburger, L. & Hastings, J. (1986). Characteristics of spouse abusers. *Journal of Interpersonal Violence, 1*, 363–373.

H.R. 740, 103d Cong., 1st Sess. (1993).

Harmon, R.B., Rosner, R., & Owens, H. (1995). Obsessional harassment and erotomania in a criminal court population. *Journal of Forensic Sciences, 40*, 188–196.

Harrell, A. & Smith, B.E. (1992). Effects of restraining orders on domestic violence victims. In: E. Buzawa. & C. Buzawa. (Eds.), *Do arrests and restraining orders work*? Newbury Park, CA: Sage.

Haw. Rev. Stat. 711–1106.5 Supp. 1992.

Healey, K. & Smith C. (with C. O'Sullivan) (1998). *Batterer intervention: Program approaches and criminal justice strategies*. Washington, D.C.: National Institute of Justice, Office of Justice Programs.

Hearing Before the Committee on the Judiciary United States Senate, 103rd Congress, 1st session on combating stalking and family violence, antistalking proposals. March 17, 1993, Serial No. J-103-5. Washington, D.C.: U.S. Government Printing Office, 1993.

Hutchison, I.W., Hirschel, J.D., & Pesackis, C.E. (1994). Family violence and police utilization. *Violence and Victims, 9* (4), 299–313.

ICLU – Your Rights in Cyberspace, http://www.law.indiana.edu

Ill. Stat. Ch 725 para. 5/110-4 Smith-Hurd, 1993.

Island D. & Letellier, P. (1991). *Men who beat the men who love them: Battered gay men and domestic violence.* New York: Haworth.

Jason, L.A., et al. (1984). Female harassment after ending a relationship: A preliminary study.
Alternative Lifestyles (6), 265–279.

joc.mit.edu/cornell/latimes

Kamphuis, J.H. & Emmelkamp, P.M.G. (2000). Stalking—a contemporary challenge for
forensic and clinical psychiatry. *British Journal of Psychiatry, 176,* 206–209.

Keilitz, S.L., et al. Civil Protection Orders: Victims' Views on Effectiveness. U.S. Dept. of
Justice, Office of Justice Programs, January 1998, www.ncjrs.org, pp. 1–3.

Kelsey, Dick, Newsbytes.com, January 27, 2000, pp. 1–2.

Kincaid, Salon.com, Aug. 24, 2000, pp. 1–5.

Klein, Andrew R. (1992). Re-abuse in a population of court-restrained male batters. In
E. Buzawa & C. Buzawa. (Eds.), *Do arrests and restraining orders work?* Newbury Park,
CA: Sage.

Kohut, H. (1972). Thoughts on narcissism and narcissistic rage (pp. 360–400). In H. Kohut
(Ed.), *Psychoanalytic Study of the Child.* New Haven, CT: Yale University Press.

Kurt, J.L. (1995). Stalking as a variant of domestic violence. *Bulletin of the American Academy
of Psychiatry and the Law, 23* (2): 219–230.

www.law.ucla.edu

Legal Pad Times.

Lester, *High Technology Careers Magazine,* 1998, pp. 1–2.

Lie, G. and Gentlewarrior, S. (1991). Intimate violence in lesbian relationships: discussion
survey findings and practice implications. *Journal of Social Service Research, 15,* 41–59.

Livingston, J.A. (1982). Responses to sexual harassment on the job: Legal, organizational and
individual actions. *Journal of Social Issues, 38* (4), 5–22.

Loper v. New York City Police Dept.

Lowney, K.S. & Best, J. (1995). Stalking strangers and lovers: Changing media typifications
of a new crime. In J. Best, (Ed.), *Images of issues—Typifying contemporary social problems,*
2nd ed., New York: Aldine de Gruyter.

McCann, J.T. (1998). Subtypes of stalking (obsessional following) in adolescents. *Journal of
Adolescence, 21* (6), 667–675.

McNamara, J.R., Ertl, M.A., Marsh, S., & Walker, S. (1997). Short-term response to counseling
and case management intervention in a domestic violence shelter. *Psychological Reports,*
81 (3, Pt. 2), 1243–1251.

McReynolds, G. (1996, January–February). The enemy you know. *Sacramento Magazine,* 22, 1,
39–42, 84.

Malley v. Briggs, 475 U.S. 335, 341 (1986).

Markowitz, F. & Felson, R. (1998). Social-demographic attitudes and violence. *Criminology,*
36 (1), 117–137.

Meloy, J. R. (1996). Stalking (obsessional following): A review of some preliminary studies.
Aggression and Violent Behavior (1), 147–162.

Meloy, J. R. (1992). Violence and erotomania (19–38). In J.R. Meloy (Ed.), *Violent attachments.*
Northvale, N.J.: Jason Aronson, Inc.

Meloy, J.R. & Gothard, S. (1995). Demographic and clinical comparison of obsessional followers and offenders with mental disorders. *American Journal of Psychiatry, 152,* 258–263.

Meloy, J.R. (1997). The clinical risk management of stalking: "Someone is watching over
me…" *American Journal of Psychotherapy, 51* (2), 174–184.

Meloy, J.R. (1999). Stalking—An old behavior, a new crime. *The Psychiatric Clinics of North America*, 22 (1), 85–99.

Meloy, J. R. (1998) *The psychology of stalking: Clinical and forensic perspectives*. San Diego: Academic Press.

Miller, G., and Maharaj, D., INFOWAR.com, January 27, 1999, pp. 1–3.

Miller, T.W. & Feibelman, N.D. (1987). Obsessional thought disturbance in a gainfully employed traumatic stress disorder patient. *Journal of Occupational Health Nursing*, 35, 69–73.

Miller, Robert N. (1993). "Stalk talk": A first look at anti-stalking legislation. *Washington and Lee Law Review*, 50, 1303–1339.

Mohandie, K. Hatcher, C., & Raymond, D. (1998). False victimization syndromes in stalking. In J.R. Meloy (Ed.), *The psychology of stalking: Clinical and forensic perspectives*. San Diego, CA: Academic Press.

Morewitz, Stephen J. (1996). *Sexual harassment and social change in American society*. Bethesda, MD: Austin and Winfield, Publishers.

Morewitz, S. (2000a). Domestic stalking and violence by ethnic/racial group: A subculture of violence approach. *Sociological Abstracts*, August Supplement, 188, 87.

Morewitz, S. (2000b). Racial/ethnic differences among domestic stalking victims involved in police contacts for domestic violence and stalking (abstract). *Proceedings of the American Association for the Advancement of Science, Pacific Division*, 10 (1), 55.

Morewitz, S. (2001a). Spouse stalking and partner sexual assaults (abstract). *Proceedings of the American Association for the Advancement of Science, Pacific Division*.

Morewitz, S. (2001b). Domestic violence and stalking during pregnancy (abstract) *Obstetrics & Gynecology, Supplement 97* (4), 53S.

Morewitz, S. (2001c). Psychosocial effects of stalking: A social problems approach. 51st Annual Meetings of the Society for the Study of Social Problems. Search Abstracts (online).

Morewitz, S. (2001d). Psychosocial factors associated with physical trauma among domestic violence victims. (abstract). *Psychosomatic Medicine*, 63 (1), 169.

Muelleman, R.L. & Feighny, K.M. (1999). Effects of an emergency department-based advocacy program for battered women on community resource utilization. *Annals of Emergency Medicine*, 33 (1), 62–66.

Mullen, P.E., et al. (1999). Study of stalkers. *American Journal of Psychiatry*, 156 (8), 1244–1249.

Mullen, P.E. & Pathe, M. (1994). The pathological extensions of love. *British Journal of Psychiatry*, 165, 614–623.

National Conference of State Legislatures, www.ncsl.org

National Council of Juvenile and Family Court Judges (1992). *Family violence: State-of-the art programs*. Reno, NV: State Justice Institute.

National Institute of Justice (1996). Domestic violence, stalking, and anti-stalking legislation: An annual report to Congress under the Violence Against Women Act. Rockville, MD: National Criminal Justice Reference Service.

National Institute of Justice (1990). *Issues and practice in criminal justice*. Rockville, MD: National Criminal Justice Reference Service.

National Institute of Justice (1993). *Project to develop a model anti-stalking code for states*. Rockville, MD: National Criminal Justice Reference Service.

National Institute of Justice (1999). *Cyberstalking: A new challenge for law enforcement and industry—A report from the Attorney General to the Vice President*. Rockville, MD: National Criminal Justice Reference Service.

National Institute of Justice (1998). *Stalking and domestic violence: The third annual report to Congress under the Violence Against Women Act*. Rockville, MD: National Criminal Justice Reference Service.

Newsbytes, 2000, pp. 1–2.

The News-Times, April 18, 1997.

New York Times on the Web, Breaking News From A.P., November 24, 2000, pp. 1–3.

Ohio Rev. Code Ann. 2903.211–.215- Baldwin Supp. 1992.

Okla. Stat. tit. 60.11 (Supp. 1993).

Palarea, R.E., Zona, M.A., Lane, J.C., & Langhinrichsen-Rohling, J. (1999). The dangerous nature of intimate relationships stalking: Threats, violence, and associated risk factors. *Behavioral Sciences and the Law, 17,* 269–283.

Pathe, M., & Mullen, P. E. (1997). The impact of stalkers on their victims, *British Journal of Psychiatry. 170,* 12–17.

Pathe, M., Mullen, P.E., & Purcell, R. (1999). Stalking: False claims of victimisation. *British Journal of Psychiatry, 174,* 170–172.

People v. Holt, 649 N.E. 2d 571 (Ill.App.Ct. 1995).

People v. White, 536 N.W.2d 876 (Mich.App.Ct.1995).

Raskin, D. E. & Sullivan, K. E. (1974). Erotomania. *American Journal of Psychiatry, 131,* 1033–1035.

Reno v. American Civil Liberties Union, 521 U.S. 844, 850–52, 870 (1997).

Richardson, Alex, ABC NEWS.com, February 13, 2001.

Roberts, A.R. & Dziegielewski, S.F. (1996). Assessment typology and intervention with the survivors of stalking. *Aggression and Violent Behavior 1* (4), 359–368.

SafetyEd International Internet Safety organization, http://www.safetyed.org

Sampson, R.J. & Laub, J.H. (1993). *Crime in the making—Pathways and turning points through life.* Cambridge, MA: Harvard University Press.

Sanchez, Jana, IDG News Service/London Bureau, June 23, 1999, p. 1.

Schwartz-Watts, D. & Morgan, D. W. (1998). Violent versus non-violent stalkers. *Journal of the American Academy of Psychiatry & the Law, 26* (2), 241–245.

Sherman, L.W. & Berk, R.A. (1984). Specific deterrent effects of arrest for domestic assault. *American Sociological Review, 49* (2), 261–272.

Sinclair, H.C. & Frieze, I. H. (2000). Initial courtship behavior and stalking: How should we draw the line? *Violence and Victims, 15* (1), 23–30.

www.soshelp.org

Spitzberg, B. Nicastro, A., & Cousins, A. (1998). Exploring the interactional phenomenon of stalking and obsessive relational intrusion. Communication Reports, *11* (1), 33–47.

State v. Holder, 418 S.E. 2d 197, 201 (N.C. 1992).

Steinmetz, S. K. (1977–1978). The battered husband syndrome. Victimology, 2, 499.

Strikis, S. (1993). Stopping stalking. *The Georgetown Law Journal,* (81), 2771–2813.

Sullivan, C.M. & Rumptz, M.H. (1994). Adjustment and needs of African-American women who utilized a domestic violence shelter. *Violence and Victims, 9* (3), 275–286.

Supreme Court of the United States, No. 96–511, http://www.ciec.org

http://thomas.loc.gov/cgi-bin/query

Tarasoff v. Regents of The University of California, 17 Cal. 3d 425, 131 Cal. Rptr. 14, 551 P. 2d 334 (1976).

Tjaden, P., Thoesnnes, N., & Allison, C. J. (2000). Comparing stalking victimization from legal and victim perspectives. *Violence and Victims, 15* (1), 7–22.

Topliffe, E. (1992). Why civil protection orders are effective remedies for domestic violence but mutual protective orders are not. *Indiana Law Journal, 67,* 1039, 1041–42.

Travis. (2000). Straw plans new tags foe stalkers and sex offenders, *The Guardian,* March 13.

Tucker, J.T. (1993). Stalking the problems with stalking laws: The effectiveness of Florida statutes section 784.048. *Florida Law Review, 45,* 609–701.

18 U.S.C. 875 (c)

18 U.S.C. 3142 (e) (1988)

18 U.S.C. 2261A (1996)

18 U.S.C. 2425 (1998)

47 U.S.C. 223

United States v. Nat'l Dairy Prods. Corp., 372 U.S. 29, 32–33 (1963).

United States of America v. Jake Baker and Arthur Gonda, U.S. District Court, Eastern District of Michigan, Southern Division.

U.S. Department of Justice (1998). Intimate partner violence. www.ojp.usdoj.gov/bjs

http://www.vtw.org

Wallace, H. & Silverman, J. (1996). Stalking and post traumatic stress syndrome. *Police Journal*, 69, 203–206.

Warr, M. (1998). Life course transitions and desistance from crime. *Criminology*, *36* (2), 183–215.

Watts v. United States, 394 U.S. 705 (1969).

www.Web-Police.org

Werner, C.M. & Haggard, L.M. (1992). Avoiding intrusions at the office: Privacy regulation on typical and high solitude days. *Basic and Applied Social Psychology*, *13*, 181–193.

West Virginia Code 61-2-9a (a) 1992.

Williams, W.L., Lane, J., and Zona, M.A. (1996). Stalking—successful intervention strategies. *The Police Chief* (Feb.), 24–26.

Wis. Stat. 29.05 (1m) (1992).

Woodall, Martha, www.standardtimes.com, April 1, 2000.

Working to Halt Online Abuse, http://haltabuse.org/laws.html

Wright, J.A., et al. Investigating stalking crimes. Journal of *Psychosocial Nursing*, *33* (9), 38–43.

Yoshihama, M. & Sorenson, S. (1994). Physical, sexual, and emotional abuse by male intimates: Experiences of women in Japan. *Violence and Victims*, *9* (1), 63–77.

Zona, M., Sharma, K., & Lane, J. (1993). A comparative study of erotomanic and obsessional subjects in a forensic sample. *Journal of Forensic Sciences*, *38*, 894–903.

Zona, M., Palarea, R., & Lane, J. (1998). Psychiatric diagnosis and the offender-victim typology of stalking (pp. 69–84). In J.R. Meloy (Ed.), The *psychology of stalking: Clinical and Forensic Perspectives*. San Diego, Academic Press.

About the Author

Dr. Stephen J. Morewitz is President of the medical–legal consulting firm Stephen J. Morewitz, Ph. D., and Associates, Buffalo Grove, Illinois, and San Francisco and Tarzana, California, which was established in 1988. Dr. Morewitz is Chair of the Crime and Delinquency Division of the Society for the Study of Social Problems. He has been on the faculty or staffs of Michael Reese Hospital and Medical Center; the University of Illinois at Chicago (UIC); the College of Medicine and School of Public Health, DePaul University; Argonne National Laboratory, Chicago, Illinois; California Hospital of Podiatric Medicine; and San Francisco General Hospital/University of California, San Francisco. He is the author of *Sexual Harassment and Social Change in American Society* (1996) and the author of over 50 articles, research abstracts, and submissions. He was elected to, Sigma Xi, the scientific research society, and to Pi Gamma Mu, the International Honor Society in Social Sciences, and is the subject of biographical record in *Who's Who in Medicine and Healthcare*. He earned his B.A. and M.A. degrees from the College of William and Mary and his Ph. D. from the University of Chicago.

Author Index

Subject Index